# Fabulous But FAKE

# Fabulous But FAKE

## THE PROFESSIONAL'S GUIDE TO FAKE ANTIQUES

## VOLUME I

BY
**NORMAN S. YOUNG**

**FAKE**
PUBLICATIONS
I N C

Young, Norman S.
Fabulous but Fake

ISBN  0-9640209-0-4

Design & Composition by Diane Moore
Editorial Assistance by Stanley Roth
Photography by Mark Merrett & Tony Story
Printing by Excelsior Printing Company
Binding by Book Press

**This book is
dedicated to my family.**

# Acknowledgments

I wish to thank the antiques dealers of the world who have knowingly or unknowingly sold me many of the fakes that are illustrated in this book. Thanks to the many people in New England and the rest of the United States who were fooled by the fakers; their encouragement was a major factor in my decision to undertake this project.

I am deeply grateful to Linda Caine from Walden Books and Donald Carpentier from Eastfield Village Historic Restoration for their valuable assistance. To the people from Chatham Installations and Welding, your help in recreating the factory manufacturing was great.

Thanks to Judith Gallo, Gail and Leigh Durland, and the Albany Auction Gallery for allowing me to photograph some of the fakes they have found.

Norman S. Young

# Contents

# Introduction

Touring New England in the 1930's with my antiques dealer parents enabled me to develop a love and appreciation for antiques. Our old Dodge touring car always came home loaded with good quality furniture and collectibles. Even back in those days there were fakes. However, the adequate supply of authentic antiques was enough to keep the demand for them repressed.

In the post-World War II years the population explosion and expanding economies produced a demand for more than our cultural past could provide. Throughout Europe and the United States a ready market developed for mass-produced fake antiques, as consumers demanded more and more quality antiques to fill their living spaces. The world's manufacturers quickly realized the tremendous profit potential of this new market and moved to create huge quantities of high quality fakes to satisfy the demand. Today this manufacturing effort has developed into an annual multi-million dollar international business of selling fakes as real antiques.

Pause for a second. Think about what makes a fake. It is a reproduction that replicates not only form, but age (wear) as well, making it difficult for anyone to tell the difference between what's real and what's not. For most of the items described in this book, remarkable effort has been taken to simulate the wear of age and to disguise modern manufacture. These fakes were meant to be sold as authentic antiques. Unscrupulous wholesale distributors and antiques dealers have been quick to capitalize on this. They put a few pieces in their warehouses and shops or consign some to their local auction sales. It is not uncommon for a $100 fake sold in this way to realize a $1000 profit for the seller. This is a common practice, not only in the United States, but throughout Europe as well.

There is nothing wrong with reproducing antiques provided they are legitimately sold as new pieces. Most of the pieces described in this book are of high quality manufacture and look like true antiques. My enthusiasm for their decorative value is evident throughtout this guide. The problem develops when they are passed off as authentic antiques and sold to an unsuspecting buyer for huge profits.

Until now, there has been almost no information to help the buyer identify one of these fakes. My "Fabulous But Fake" guide will fill that gap, providing a single information source for details on many of the world's fake antiques. The antiques trade will find this guide invaluable in identifying fakes. It can be very helpful to decorators as a source book for period looking pieces at a fraction of an original's cost. Consumers will now be able to make informed decisions.

Whether you are religious in your pursuit of original antiques or just someone who enjoys the re-creation of antique style settings, this guide could save you a lot of money and anguish. Remember that Fabulous Fakes are so good, they can even fool the experts. Follow my rules and avoid overpaying for what you buy.

# Common Sense Buying Practices

**1.** When you have made what you think is a great discovery, **keep cool.** Your best judgment comes with a calm, common sense evaluation of your find. If your discovery matches one the fakes shown in this book, assume that it is a fake unless there is proof to the contrary. With thousands of fakes in circulation for each authentic piece, your chances of discovering a real antique are low.

**2. Think about the form of your find and how it was manufactured.** Early antiques were made by craftsmen and artisans who incorporated their artistic abilities into their work. Later, product manufacturers paid more attention to commercial success, with a resulting decline in artistic quality.
Manufacturing techniques can tell you a lot about the age of your find. If it was gas-welded or electric-welded, chances are it was made in the twentieth century. Earlier production would have used techniques such as forge-welding or soldering.

**3. Examine the surface of the piece closely.** You can tell a lot about the age of something by the marks that you see or don't see. On normal wear surfaces you should find a very smooth, abraded appearance on all the high spots, which is normal for something that is old. Heavy, coarse scratches should be viewed with suspicion. Heavy grind marks and weld undercutting also indicate later manufacture. Be wary of cracked paint finishes; they are very easily faked.

**4. On expensive items, a sound provenance is a must.** You must be able to verify the source and real history of the piece. Too many times colorful stories have been made up to enhance its value.

**5.** *The old adage of "get it in writing" still applies.* The dealer or person from whom you buy the antiques should be willing to supply the necessary documentation to guarantee its age and provenance. With this information in hand, you will have legal recourse if it proves to be false.

**6.** Although you can't always pick the circumstances under which your purchases are made, it is still best to **know the dealer or person from whom you buy.** The seller's experience and reputation should be considered when making a purchase decision.

**7.** *Be wary of anyone who takes only cash.* It is best to pay by credit card or personal check. If, after making your purchase, you find that it was purposely misrepresented, you have several days to stop payment and return the piece.

**8.** *Caveat Emptor.* Let the buyer beware of goods sold through local auction houses and sale rooms. Many times dealers consign their mistakes, damaged pieces and fakes to these sales in the hope of making a killing or recovering their losses.

**9.** *Don't be afraid to buy a* "Fabulous Fake" *as a fake.* They make good decorating sense. You get the replication of design and age without the high price tag of the original. Consider the work of Wallace Nutting. The fakes he made years ago are very collectible today and are sold in antiques shops.

# How To Use This Guide

The primary use of my guide will be as a reference to what has been faked, allowing you to make informed purchases and avoid the mistake of overpaying. Another use will be to evaluate your past purchases and determine whether they are real antiques or fakes.

Each fake in this guide has its own item number and individual data sheet. The information on the data sheet has been divided into four sections of text along with a full color photograph of each object.

The photographs and size information relate to fakes only. No authentic antiques are shown.

## Data Sheet Information

The first section of text provides historical background and bits of information about the appearance and use of the original antique. Information on contemporary use and decorating ideas also will be found in this section.

The second section, Construction, provides detailed information on the manufacture of fakes for comparison purposes. The first step used in identifying a mass-produced fake is to compare your piece's dimensions to the known fake's dimensions.

The third section, Finish, describes the protective coatings used for the aging process. They simulate the wear and corrosion of an authentic antique, successfully removing or masking many of the marks of modern manufacture.

The fourth section, Fake Tip-off, provides specific information to complete your evaluation of authenticity. If your piece matches the one on the data sheet, chances are you have a fake.

A summary has been provided at the end of each chapter. It contains my general views on common features of the fakes within the section. If the Fake Tip-offs are common for all of the section's fakes, they will be found in the summary rather than under each data sheet.

**Warning** - Many of the fake tip-offs are discrepancies that could be overcome with a little more care and expense. If this guide creates a more knowledgable consumer, the fakers will probably respond by improving their techniques. A good general rule to follow: if the dimensions and description match the fakes, do not buy it as antique without solid proof.

**Fabulous Fakes Price List**

In the process of researching the fakes described in this guide, it was necessary for me to buy most of the items and track down their sources. Since a legitimate price for the Fabulous Fakes, as reproductions, is necessary if the reader of this guide is to avoid paying the price of a real antique, I have provided a current price list in the pocket inside the back cover.

This research has also made it possible for me to supply some of these fakes at this legitimate price. If you want to buy one of the fakes described in this guide, information on availability and  ordering is provided.

# Modern Technology

Understanding how fakes are made and the manufacturing processes used in their production will help dispel the illusion that masks their true age.

Every item illustrated in this guide has been manufactured using modern machinery and production techniques. The fakers realized early on that the ancient way of making a piece would not be profitable even with a cheap labor source.

Modern technology and equipment have made it possible. All the simulated iron devices used electric welding in place of the time-consuming method of hand forging welds. The electric welding machinery commonly used in this manufacture is a wire feed type. Fine diameter steel welding wire wound on large spools is used as an electrode and fed through an insulated handle to the weld joint. When touched to the metal in the joint, it immediately melts, forming a metal bond. These welds are created with low heat and result in fine, accurately placed deposits of additional metal to the joint.

It is here that the fakers can not completely duplicate a hand-forged weld. The electric weld, in addition to melting the base metal of the fake, also adds additional metal to the joint.

*Modern electric welding equipment.*

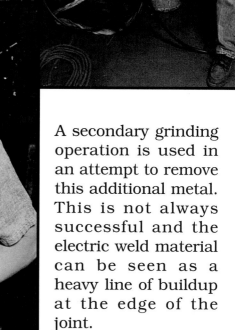

A secondary grinding operation is used in an attempt to remove this additional metal. This is not always successful and the electric weld material can be seen as a heavy line of buildup at the edge of the joint.

*Hand-held electric grinder.*

*Found on a Long Island, New York, construction site, a verified old iron toaster supplies us with a picture of what a true hand forged weld looks like.*

*This is a faked forged weld joint. It has been made using electric welding and finish grinding. You can see the buildup of electric weld material highlighted across the top of the photograph.*

Both pieces of material in a hand forged weld are heated to a near white-hot temperature. They are then placed together and hammered on the joint, welding together completely across the joint surface.

In order to show what a faked weld looks like on the inside, I got my nerve up and cut through one of the game racks shown on data sheet #107. The faked forged weld that you see in the following illustration used modern electric welding on its exterior surface. I have cut partially through the joint with a hacksaw and bent the cut piece back to show the lack of weld penetration. The two bent outside edges show bonding and display the unwelded material surface of the detail part.

*Cutaway of fake forged weld.*

## Plastic Body Filler

On three dimensional figures of both wood and metal construction, another space age product speeds the production of fakes. A two-part polyester resin plastic body filler is used to create smooth body contours. It is simple to use and sands to a feather edge. On genuine antiques, the base material of the piece would have been sculpted to obtain the necessary contours. Look for the telltale grey of the plastic material in cracks and surface scratches.

# I. Silhouette Weathervanes

## Contents

# Eagle Weathervane

**1**

An impressive, flat profile of an eagle ready to strike, this piece represents the shadow image of a late 1800's full bodied weathervane.

*Front Side Illustrated*

**Overall Height: 23** $^3/_4$"      **Overall Length: 38** $^1/_4$"
**Sheet Thickness:** $^1/_{16}$"      **Strapping Size:** $^1/_{16}$" **x** $^5/_8$"

Construction: The complex eagle shape is cut out by hand from flat, mild steel sheet. Rough hammered steel strapping, riveted to the back side of the eagle, forms the pivot supports and adds additional strength. A great touch of realism is obtained by hammering the rivet heads and tails into the flat surface of the weathervane.

Finish: A heavy coat of red primer paint with a special cracking ingredient and a final top coat of black, almost grungy, paint are applied by cross-brushing. A little chipped paint and corrosion makes this fake believable as a real antique.

# Dove and Arrow Weathervane 2

A dove of peace standing on an arrow of war reflects the mood of the United States in the post-Revolution years. The flat sheet metal construction and simple form make this a very attractive weathervane.

*Front Side Illustrated*

**Overall Height: 16"**
**Overall Length: 30 ⁵/₈"**
**Sheet Thickness: ¹/₁₆"**
**Strapping Size: ¹/₁₆" x ¹/₂"**

Construction: Two pieces of mild sheet steel riveted together give this vane its form. Steel strapping riveted to the back side of the vane provides strength and pivot support. The location of the strapping can be determined by following the rivet pattern in the illustration. Look at the rivet heads: there is almost no distortion. This is due in part to the modern equipment used in the manufacturing process.

Finish: The arrow, painted black-green over red primer, shows wear on the rivets and bits of chipped paint. Red primer is left on the dove and the entire weathervane is coated with a sooty finish-- a great look.

# Dove Weathervane

*Back Side Illustrated*

**Overall Height: 24"**
**Sheet Thickness: $^1/_{16}$"**

**Overall Length: 30 $^3/_8$"**
**Strapping Size: $^1/_{16}$" x $^1/_2$"**

George Washington, the first president of the United States, chose a dove carrying an olive branch to fly above Mount Vernon. Although this fake was made in the mirror image of the original, it still sends the same message.

Construction: Four pieces of hand cut mild steel sheet make up the body of this vane. They are riveted together with crude overlapping seams. Steel strapping, hand forged and riveted to its back side, adds strength. The two pivot supports, made of formed sheet metal, are riveted in place. The eye detail is a hole cut through the sheet metal.

Finish: The completed weathervane is pre-corroded, coated with red primer and given a sooty black top coat of finish.

# Locomotive Weathervane 4

The weathered outline of an 1860's locomotive has a universal appeal to railroad buffs around the world. This re-creation is no exception. Smoke billowing from its stack, an engineer at the throttle, it presents an almost moving picture of an "iron horse."
The pivot point on the weathervane is situated so that the locomotive will always head into the wind and the smoke from its stack will be directionally correct.

Construction: The locomotive shape is cut out by hand from a piece of steel sheet. Because of the thin sections of the vane cut-out, a web of steel strapping is riveted to the back side to provide additional strength and a secure pivot support. The strap ends are finish ground almost to a point and distressed slightly, giving a hand forged appearance. The irregular spacing of the spokes in the two front wheels seems to give credence to its claim of age.

Finish: Black grungy paint is liberally applied over a cracked red primer. A little accelerated surface wear and chipping of paint complete the manufacturing process.

*Back Side Illustrated*

**Overall Height: 20"**
**Sheet Thickness:** 1/16"

**Overall Length: 45** 3/8"
**Strapping Size:** 1/16" x 1/2"

# Regal Cockerel Weathervane 5

A flat profile with six feathers and a regal looking, crown shaped comb make this barnyard friend an easy one to remember. The fabrication of its many sheet steel pieces has been so crudely done that it looks like a "make do", to use up small pieces of material left over from other projects.

*Back Side Illustrated*

**Overall Height: 21 3/8"**
**Overall Length: 21 1/4"**
**Sheet Thickness: .040"**
**Strapping Size: 1/16" x 1/2"**

Construction: Riveted pieces of mild steel sheet, crudely shaped, form the cockerel body. Strength and rigidity are increased by riveting five pieces of steel strapping to the back side of the vane. The pivot supports formed from sheet steel are riveted in place. All the strapping is cosmetically hammered to simulate hand forging. The rivets are over formed and squashed flat to provide an additional primitive effect.

Finish: The sheet steel surface of this weathervane is coated with a flaking red primer. A final top coating of a sooty film has given it a well-used look.

*Front Side Illustrated*

**Overall Height: 28"**
**Sheet Thickness:** 1/16"

**Overall Length: 32** 3/8"
**Strapping Size:** 1/16" **x** 1/4"

# Red Cockerel Weathervane                    6

The original of this cockerel weathervane probably graced the spire of a church. The cockerel traditionally served as a reminder of Peter's denial of Christ and a warning not to follow his example. This one has been reproduced in a true folk art form.

Construction: Made from three pieces of mild steel sheet riveted together, it is hand cut to attain the form and feeling of the original weathervane. Steel strapping, riveted around the curved body outline, provides additional strength and rigidity needed to withstand the effects of the weather. The delicate tail feathers also have a piece of riveted, curved strapping added for strength. The pivot supports and the single leg of the cockerel, formed from steel strapping, are riveted in place.

Finish: The weathervane surface is artificially corroded and then painted with a finish coat of bright red paint.

**Recycled Scrap**

*In the center section of the body there is a noticeable crease in the sheet iron. I suspect that recycled scrap material is being used. In addition to the hand hammering that is evident in this close-up view, it is important to consider the surface finish of the sheet metal. The obvious pitting of the metal is a good example of a faked weathered surface.*

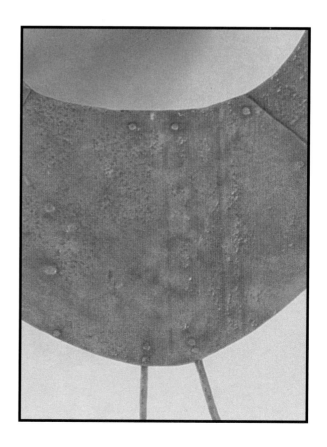

# Cock Weathervane

*Back Side Illustrated*

**Overall Height: 22"**
**Sheet Thickness:** ¹/₁₆"

**Overall Length: 26 ¹/₂"**
**Strapping Size:** ¹/₁₆" x ¹/₄"

This uncommon form of weathercock may have been copied from footless medieval styles. The symmetrical tail feathers and arched neck balance the plump body, giving this bird its delightful character.

Construction: Cut from three pieces of mild steel sheet, this vane was crafted with great attention to straight seam edges and smooth flowing curves. You will notice that even the reinforcing strapping looks machine formed. The sheet metal and strapping are riveted together with great care and precision. Two formed pieces of sheet steel, riveted to the back side, provide the pivot support. Highlights of a wing are cutouts in the bird's body. Notice the rivets shown on the right hand feather of the wing. This is a common method used by the fakers to correct burnouts caused by the corroding process or holes drilled by mistake.

Finish: Black grungy paint applied over red primer and a well-corroded surface are the finishing touches for this bird.

# Bishop's Weathervane 8

*Back Side Illustrated*

**Overall Height: 24 $^3/_8$"**
**Overall Length: 20 $^1/_4$"**
**Banner Height: 6"**
**Banner Length: 16 $^3/_8$"**
**Sheet Thickness: .040"**
**Strapping Size: $^1/_{16}$" x $^1/_2$"**

Rooster weathervanes historically signalled a religious presence and this one is probably no different. The original weathercock could have been mounted atop a church spire, prominently displaying the bishop's symbol to the world.

Construction; Four pieces of hand cut mild steel sheet make up this bird. Assembly is accomplished by overlapping riveted seams. A steel strapping framework riveted to the back side provides additional strength. The pivot supports are sheet metal, riveted in place. Some hand forging and overhammered rivets combine to give this vane a great aged look.

Finish: After assembly, our red rooster is unceremoniously given a corrosive bath and an alligatored, pebbly red primer coat of paint. A sooty top finish has produced a nineteenth-century look.

*Back Side Illustrated*

**Overall Height: 29 <sup>3</sup>/4"**
**Overall Length: 22"**
**Sheet Thickness: <sup>1</sup>/16"**
**Strapping Size: 1" x <sup>1</sup>/16"**

# Albany Cockerel Weathervane 9

The original of this weathervane was brought to the United States from Holland in the year 1656. One of the first vanes of the walking rooster type, it was mounted atop the First Reformed Church in Albany, New York. There are several differences between this copy and the original. The upper pivot support on the original was a much larger piece of sheet metal and was fastened with four rivets. Also, on the tail of the original there is a support strap riveted across the top four feathers.

Construction: Hand cut out of flat steel sheet, its six pieces are riveted together with roughly formed overlapping seams. Three pieces of steel strapping, riveted to the back side across the body seams, provide additional strength. Pivot supports, made of two small pieces of sheet metal, are riveted in place.

Finish: The sheet metal parts are pre-corroded and coated with red primer. A top coat of black paint finishes it off. Bits of flaking paint and a little wear give it an amazingly original-looking finish.

# Game Cock  Weathervane

*Back Side Illustrated*

**Overall Height: 18** $^1/_4$"
**Overall Length: 23** $^1/_4$"
**Sheet Thickness:** $^1/_{16}$"
**Strapping Size:** $^7/_{16}$" **x** $^1/_8$"

"Le coq rouge" is a representation of a gamecock in a rather primitive form. Its heart cutout, single leg and square cut comb are distinctive characteristics of this weathervane.

Construction:  Crudely cutting the pieces out of mild sheet steel gives this fake its eighteenth-century manufactured look. The six pieces of sheet are riveted together with hand formed overlapping seams. A riveted hand-forged iron strapping framework on the back side reinforces the vane. Pivot supports are formed pieces of sheet steel riveted in place. The rivet fasteners have been overhammered and squashed flat into the surface of the vane.

Finish: The finish produced on this weathervane is truly exceptional. A red primer coat applied to a well-corroded sheet metal surface almost makes this fake look older than the original.

# Spurred Cock Weathervane   **11**

*Back Side Illustrated*

One can find many features of American Shem Drowne's cockerel of 1722 in our bird. Its single spurred leg and high plumage make a dramatic statement in the sky.

**Overall Height: 26"**
**Overall Length: 31 1/2"**
**Sheet Thickness: 1/16"**
**Strapping Size: 1/16" x 1/2"**

Construction: The crude rooster form is hand-cut out of thin mild sheet steel, with a steel strapping framework riveted to its back side and pivot supports providing additional strength. By hand hammering the strapping, the false image of age is enhanced.

Finish: A black, slightly wrinkled paint finish is applied over a coat of red primer. A little paint chipping has revealed the rusted mill finish of the rolled steel. This finish completes the deception.

# Beef Butcher's Weathervane

*Front Side Illustrated*

**Overall Height:** 27"
**Sheet Thickness:** $1/32$"

**Overall Length:** 24 $7/8$"
**Strapping Size:** $1/16$" x $1/2$"

A beef butcher's weathervane copied from an old trade sign presents an oversize, almost chunky representation of the butcher's trade tools.

Construction: Two pieces of hand-cut mild steel sheet, riveted together with an overlapping seam, form this vane. A framework of steel strapping is riveted to its back side to provide additional strength and pivot supports.

Finish: A black, slightly wrinkled paint finish is applied over a coat of red primer. A little paint chipping reveals the sheet metal pre-corroded surface.

# Pork Butcher's Weathervane 13

This pork butcher's weathervane is derived from an old trade sign. The naive and primitive pig, combined with a butcher's trade tools, makes this a truly wonderful form.

*Back Side Illustrated*

**Overall Height: 23"**
**Sheet Thickness:** $^1/_{32}$"

**Overall Length: 30** $^1/_2$"
**Strapping Size:** $^1/_{16}$" x $^5/_8$"

Construction: This vane is hand-cut from a single sheet of thin mild steel. A framework of steel strapping riveted to the back side provides the strength necessary to withstand the weather. The strapping and its rivet fasteners are crudely hammered into the vane. The two pivot supports, formed from the saw straps, are located just to the right of the center member.

Finish: A black, cracked and pebbly paint over red primer provides a realistic aged appearance. Chipped paint has exposed the corroded surface of the vane material.

### Deceptive Corrosion

*A close-up look at the pig shows detail that is hard to imagine on something that is this new. The forged support bar across the pig's feet is truly handmade, complete with rivets that have been anvil-flattened. The steel parts of the weathervane have been creatively corroded prior to painting, as the brown areas on the pig's snout and back reflect. The black, grungy paint has been applied to simulate many years accumulation. The cracking and chipping complete the false image. An enlargement of the finish surface can be found inside the front and back covers of this book.*

# Moonshine Weathervane    **14**

Two "country gentlemen" in period clothes, portrayed sampling the output of their still with oversize cups, make quite a different type of weathervane. In a folksy way, it could have been a political statement for that time.

*Back Side Illustrated*

**Overall Height: 21 ⁷/₈"**
**Sheet Thickness: ¹/₃₂"**

**Overall Length: 27 ⁵/₈"**
**Strapping Size: ¹/₁₆" x ¹/₂"**

Construction: This vane is hand-cut from a single mild steel sheet. In spite of its extremely complex shape, good facial and clothing detail has been attained. Steel strapping, riveted to the vane's back side, provides additional strength and stiffness. Two pieces of that strapping bent into loops provide the pivot support. Hammered rivets give an original condition look.

Finish: The pre-rusted weathervane with its coating of pebbly red primer and top coat of grungy, black paint delivers a deceptively aged appearance. The pieces are shipped from the manufacturer unwrapped, receiving dents and chipped paint that make them even more believable as antiques.

# Centaur Weathervane

*Front Side Illustrated*

**Overall Height: 23"**
**Sheet Thickness:** $^1/_{16}$"

**Overall Length: 33 $^3/_4$"**
**Strapping Size:** $^1/_{16}$" x $^1/_2$"

The mythological centaur Chiron, or Sagittarius, was copied as a flat form weathervane from the full-bodied vanes of the late 1800's.

Construction: This interesting shape of half horse and half man is hand-cut from a single sheet of thin mild steel. For additional strength, a framework of roughly hammered steel strapping is riveted on the back side of the vane. The crudely formed rivet heads and tails complement the overall primitive appearance. The pivot support is made from a piece of sheet steel and riveted to the back side. Deformation under the rivet heads supplies additional character.

Finish: A black grungy paint, applied over an alligatored red primer leaves you with the impression of bona fide age. Chip off a little paint to show an underneath surface of rusted metal... does that look antique!

# Kentucky Weathervane 16

A race horse named Kentucky served as the model for this weathervane. Prominent in the 1860's, this horse won twenty consecutive races and the first Travers Stakes at Saratoga Springs, New York. In flat sheet metal a shadow image of that moment in racing history has been recreated.

*Front Side Illustrated*

**Overall Height: 23"**
**Sheet Thickness:** $^1/_{16}$"

**Overall Length: 38** $^1/_2$"
**Strapping Size:** $^1/_{16}$" x $^1/_2$"

Construction: The vane, hand-cut from a single sheet of mild steel, has its smooth lines unbroken by material seams. To obtain the strength necessary to withstand the forces of nature, a framework of steel strapping is riveted to the back side of the vane. It should be noted that the pivot supports riveted on the back side are located close to the figure's center line. This prevents it from moving in the wind. Evidently the manufacturer of this fake did not understand how weathervanes operate.

Finish: After a rust-inducing corrosive process, the weathervane receives a coat of red primer and a topping of black, grungy paint, enough to keep "Ole Kentucky" running for years.

# Black Hawk Weathervane

It is probable that the full-bodied horse weathervane, Black Hawk, manufactured by Harris & Company, an American firm of the late 1800's, served as the model for this vane.

Construction: Six pieces of hand-cut mild sheet steel make up the vane body. They are riveted together with 7/8" overlapping joints. Steel strapping is riveted to the back side of the vane to gain additional strength. Pivot supports are formed sheet metal, riveted in place. Hammered rivet heads serve to heighten the realism.

Finish: The vane is put through an accelerated corrosive process that creates a delightfully rusted surface. A red primer is then applied with a light top coat of grungy black paint. Bits of flaking paint, red primer showing - "Voila" - history is recreated.

**Overall Height:** 19 1/2"
**Overall Length:** 28 1/4"
**Sheet Thickness:** 1/16"
**Strapping Size:** 1/16" x 1/2"

*Front Side Illustrated*

# Horse & Rider Weathervane 18

*Front Side Illustrated*

**Overall Height: 28 ³/₄"**
**Sheet Thickness: ¹/₁₆"**

**Overall Length: 28 ³/₈"**
**Strapping Size: ¹/₁₆" x ¹/₂"**

Here is great folksy silhouette of a horse and rider similar to some full-bodied vanes by the American company, A. L. Jewell.

Construction: The large size of this vane was no hindrance to its being fabricated from one sheet of mild steel. Hand cutting allowed good detail to be obtained. A steel strapping framework riveted to the back side provides additional strength and pivot supports. The eye detail is accomplished by cutting a hole through the sheet metal. Hand forging of the strapping helps create a feeling of age.

Finish: The sheet metal surface, painted with a brown primer and finished with a dark green paint under a crackly black top coat, delivers the fake vane's look of authenticity. A little paint has chipped off here and there, exposing rusted sheet metal.

# Foxhound Weathervane

This flat sheet metal weathervane was originally made by the American company of L.W. Cushing as a full-bodied vane of a foxhound in a running form.

*Front Side Illustrated*

**Overall Height: 13 $^1/_8$"**
**Sheet Thickness:** $^1/_{16}$"

**Overall Length: 37 $^1/_4$"**
**Strapping Size:** $^1/_{16}$" x $^5/_8$"

Construction: It is made of three pieces of mild sheet steel riveted together. There is an overlapping small material seam, located at the base of the tail, and a larger one, just below the tail, joining the back legs to the body. A thin steel strap has been riveted to the back side, along with a piece of formed sheet metal for a pivot support. The rivets and the pivot support are rough hammer forged to simulate early manufacturing techniques.

Finish: Here we go again... that same black grungy paint over red primer. It makes a terrific finish that looks as old as the hills.

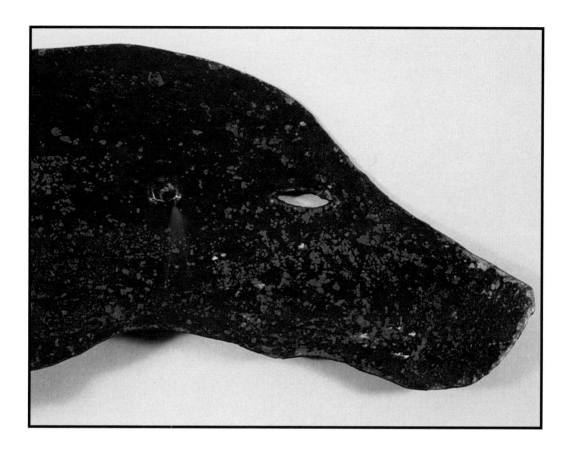

### Illusion of Age

*This picture illustrates just how well the illusion of age has been produced. The pre-corroded steel sheet metal presents a century old look of rust pitting. A few well placed hammer blows have added dents and distortion to the sheet surface. The rivet heads and tails have been anvil flattened. Red primer, liberally applied, with a top coat of grungy black paint finishes the look. The black paint is processed so that when it dries, bits flake off to give the weathervane a wonderfully aged appearance.*

# Blacksmith Weathervane 20

*Front Side Illustrated*

**Overall Height: 19 ¹/₂"**
**Sheet Thickness: .040"**

**Overall Length: 39"**
**Strapping Size: ¹/₂" x ¹/₈"**

Embodying a popular theme of the early 1800's, this weathervane portrays one of the prominent craftsmen of the period, along with his willing charge.

Construction: By hand cutting from sheet steel, many small details are achieved. The man's face, the horseshoe on the anvil and the tail of the horse are good examples of this. Steel strapping, riveted on the vane's backside, provides the necessary rigidity. On this weathervane round head rivets are used, with no attempt to change their form. Steel strapping pivot supports are located on the backside of the horse's head and the lower ground bar.

Finish: Black grungy paint over a cracked red primer, bits of paint chipped off, especially on the round rivet heads, finish this fake.

# Codfish Weathervane

The codfish has long been considered a symbol of Christianity. It is a type of weathervane found on buildings along the New England coast. This fake is an accurate replica of an old handmade codfish. Its aged appearance and hand-forged-looking details have made it almost believable as an antique.

*Back Side Illustrated*

**Overall Height: 14"**
**Sheet Thickness:** $1/16$"

**Overall Length: 38** $1/4$"
**Strapping Size:** $1/16$" x $1/2$"

Construction: The codfish body, cut, from two pieces of mild steel sheet, is joined together by an irregularly cut, overlapping riveted seam. Both the rivets and the metal seam are cosmetically overhammered in order to simulate old hand forging techniques. Steel strapping, riveted along the center line, gives it additional strength. A bent piece of sheet steel with two holes, riveted in place, serves as the weathervane pivot. The fish scales, gills, eye, mouth and tail web are openings cut through the sheet metal.

Finish: The pre-corroded metal surface of the fish is given a coat of red primer and finished with a top coat of black, grungy paint. The red primer has an additive that allows it to congeal and crack upon drying. The resulting finish looks as if it has been exposed to the elements for years.

# Butterfly Weathervane

Insects are a popular theme for weathervanes. A butterfly provides the theme for this vane, appropriately symbolizing its wind driven operation.

*Front Side Illustrated*

**Overall Height: 23"**
**Sheet Thickness: .040**

**Overall Length: 27 ⁵/₈"**
**Strapping Size: ¹/₁₆" x ¹/₂"**

Construction: The vane is fabricated from four pieces of mild sheet steel, riveted together, along with pieces of steel strapping behind the vertical and horizontal bars. Notice the interlocking legs and the antennae, captured by strapping. Pivot supports are bent sheet metal, riveted in place. The eye and wing details are simply holes cut through the sheet metal.

Finish: The vertical and horizontal bars are red primed with a black top coat of paint. The butterfly is red primed with another red as a top coat. With its mildly distressed sheet metal surface and bits of chipped paint, this vane might pass vetting at a major sale room.

# Goat Weathervane

*Front Side Illustrated*

**Overall Height: 25** $^{1}/_{2}$"
**Sheet Thickness:** $^{1}/_{16}$"

**Overall Length: 32"**
**Strapping Size:** $^{1}/_{16}$" **x** $^{1}/_{2}$"

A silhouette weathervane of above average quality, this "old goat," chipped, battered and dented, looks about as real as you can get.

Construction: Hand cutting from a single steel sheet allowed the faker freedom to create details that would otherwise be unattainable. A framework of steel strapping on the back side provides strength and the pivot supports necessary to keep the vane swinging in the wind. A hole cut through the vane provides the eye detail.

Finish: Black grungy paint serves as the top coat for the pre-corroded and red primed sheet metal surface.

# Civil War Soldier Weathervane

Silhouette weathervanes abound in many forms, some colorfully decorated. Our subject, an American Civil War soldier in drab green, is an adaptation of a vane that is privately owned.

Construction: Cut from a single thin steel sheet, this vane gets our attention with its crisp, clean profile. Wide steel strapping supports the gun and soldier in their vertical stance. Pivot supports and the rest of the strapping are riveted in place. An interesting feature of this adaptation is the way details are created. They are simply holes cut through the vane.

Finish: The sheet metal on this vane exhibits an evenly corroded surface. Red primer is applied along with a top coat of drab green paint, resulting in a finish that is remarkably even and would probably provide a good base for the addition of Union or Confederate colors.

**Overall Height: 29 ³/₄"**
**Overall Length: 22"**
**Sheet Thickness: ¹/₁₆"**
**Strapping Size: ¹/₁₆" x 1"**

*Back Side Illustrated*

# Painted Angel Gabriel Weathervane 25

*Front Side Illustrated*

**Overall Height: 48"**

**Sheet Thickness:** $1/16$"

**Overall Length: 29 $1/4$"**

The angel Gabriel, according to Christian belief, heralds the coming resurrection by the blowing of a horn. This rendition of that event is handmade of sheet metal and painted on both sides.

Construction: This weathervane, made of six pieces of mild sheet steel, is a riveted assembly. A framework of steel strapping riveted to the back side provides additional strength. Two pieces of formed sheet steel, riveted in place, form the pivot supports. The strapping framework and attaching rivets exhibit very little age distressing.

Finish: Bright new paint and a relatively clean material surface are characteristics of this fake weathervane. Close attention to the paint detail and shading has made this a very colorful image.

# Angel Gabriel Weathervane

*Front Side Illustrated*

**Overall Height: 29", with the pivot vertical**
**Overall Length: 41", with the pivot vertical**
**Sheet Thickness: ¹/₁₆"**

Advertised as real, with a $20,000 pre-sale estimate by an American auction gallery, this fake angel weathervane has caused more problems for legitimate dealers than any other. The manufacture of its form so closely follows the pattern of original construction that determining the authenticity of the piece is very difficult.
It has an aged surface that is wonderful. The surface of its metal material has been heavily rusted and pitted. It has the crude riveted joints and minor repairs that one would expect to find on an old weathervane.

Construction: The weathervane's body is cut to size from five pieces of mild sheet steel, which are riveted together. Four additional pieces of sheet steel, 1/16" thick, have been formed into ribs that are riveted to its back side. They provide the additional strength and rigidity necessary to withstand the elements. A thin piece of steel strapping is riveted to the back of the horn for additional strength. Two pivot brackets are riveted under the ends of the vertical rib. The rivet joints on the body of the angel are overlapping, with deformed rivets. The eye hole is a hole cut in the sheet metal. The two holes in the pivot brackets are 9/16" in diameter.

Finish: The sheet steel and strapping are pre-corroded before the start of manufacture. This pitted and rusted surface receives a heavy coating of orange-red primer. Bits of paint chipped off during shipping and a little grungy dirt put the finishing touches on one of the best fake finishes I have ever seen.

## Mystery Solved

Why does the male angel Gabriel have a female shape? The "breast" is actually the end of the angel's shoulder. The arm holding the horn should have continued down to meet the shoulder, terminating in a riveted joint. The missing piece was broken off on the original weathervane and the fakers, not realizing a piece was missing, copied it exactly. If that is so, it stands to reason that other angel Gabriel weathervanes with a female form were copied from the original damaged weathervane.

*The sheet steel of this weathervane has been cut from pre-corroded stock. It is very apparent as shown here on the backside of the angel's wings. They have an entirely different corrosion pattern than the rest of the body. The material edge is the point at which the pattern changes.*

# Standing Angel Gabriel Weathervane    27

*Back Side Illustrated*

**Overall Height: 28 $^1/_2$"**
**(with the pivot vertical)**
**Overall Length: 28 $^1/_4$"**
**(with the pivot vertical)**
**Sheet Thickness: $^1/_{16}$"**
**Strapping Size: $^3/_{32}$" x 1"**

The standing angel Gabriel
is another marvelous
weathervane. It has a great
folksy look and its production
detailing creates an antique
appearance that can fool experts.

Construction: Four pieces of mild sheet
steel, cut to size and riveted together with
overlapping joints, form the body of this
weathervane. A piece of sheet steel, formed into a pivot support, is
riveted in place at the lower edge of Gabriel's tunic. Steel strapping,
with both the edges and the ends ground to produce a curved top

surface, is riveted to the back side of the weathervane. Some cosmetic hammering has been done to the top surface of the strapping to give it a hand-forged look. The eye and eyebrow are holes cut through the sheet steel.

Finish: The metal surface of this piece does not appear to be corroded beyond normal mill scale. A first coat of red primer and a rough brush coat of brown primer serves as the final finish. The finish has blistered and peeled, giving the weathervane a naturally aged appearance.

### Where's the Wear

*About the only thing wrong with the credibility of this vane is the wear that should appear on the pivot surface. There is none at all. The opening of this pivot is perfectly round and does not show any indication of the distortion or wear that would normally be associated with an old weathervane.*

# Spyglass Weathervane

Originally this weathervane was found as a pub sign in a Baltic seaport. The woman, in her bright and colorful costume, seems to be searching the stormy sea in a graceful and beautifully reproduced image. The close attention to detail and the accuracy of painting has produced an almost three-dimensional feeling to the figure.

*Front Side Illustrated*

**Overall Height: 32 ³/₄"**
**Overall Length: 17 ¹/₂"**
**Sheet Thickness: ¹/₁₆"**

Construction: This weathervane, hand-cut from six pieces of pre-corroded sheet steel, is riveted together with overlapping joints. The rivet heads are hand hammered, resulting in a delightfully irregular shape. The buttons on the jacket are simply crude holes punched through the vane. The heavy sheet thickness and narrow profile eliminate the need for any strapping reinforcements. Sheet metal pivot supports are riveted to the back side.

Finish: After assembly, the weathervane has been lightly corroded and red primed. The finish colors are then artfully applied... and "WOW".

This is a higher quality fake than most of the other weathervanes illustrated in this guide. However, the fake tip-offs contained in the summary at the end of this chapter still apply.

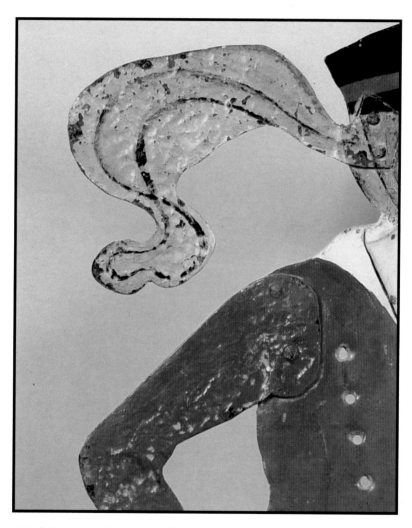

### *Evidence of Corrosion*
*The overlapping seams on the sheet metal demonstrate the attention to detail the faker gave this weathervane. The duplication of original manufacturing methods is remarkable. Look at the deep corrosion cratering on her arm and scarf. It looks like the result of years of exposure to wind and rain.*

# Weathervane Summary & Fake Tip-offs

You will find it very difficult to recognize the recent constuction of a weathervane made by the fake manufacturers. Their products often fool even the experts. The prime reason for this difficulty is that there is only one mechanical wear surface on a vane and that is the pivot. All the other surfaces receive wear from their exposure to the weather, one of the easiest conditions to fake.

All of the silhouette weathervanes illustrated in this guide have had their metal surfaces artificially corroded and aged using mass production techniques. Cracked painted finishes, easily produced with special paint additives, have been used to create the final illusion of age.

Generally you need one or more indicators on which to base your judgment of a silhouette weathervane. The following tip-offs provide information on common fake manufacturing procedures that should be helpful in determining whether you have a fake or a real antique.

## Fake Tip-offs

**1.** All of the fake weathervane shapes have been traced from actual antiques or copied from photographs. Production tracing templates have probably been made. The use of these templates would result in standard sizes for all production fakes. Measure the size of the piece in question and compare the size to its illustrated known fake counterpart. If the size matches, it is a good indication that the piece is a fake. But that by itself is not enough to label the piece as a fake. Combined with any of the other tip-offs, it is.

**2.** Remember that the original antique forms of the fake weathervanes in this chapter were one of a kind.

**3.** The illustrated fakes have common mechanical features, such as overlapping joint construction, rivets, pivot support design and material size.

**4.** On authentically old weathervanes, the bearing surfaces of the pivot should exhibit worn thin sections, metal galling and rolled over metal edges caused by the rotation action of the wind. None of the weathervanes appearing in this guide have that type of wear reproduced on their pivot surfaces. The detail photograph of the #27 Angel Gabriel shows the typically non-worn pivot condition of a fake.

**5.** The painted finish of color or faded black over cracked red primer is a trademark of this group of fakes. If your vane has an uncracked black finish over this type of primer, be suspicious.

*A word of caution is needed here. Remember that it is very easy to coat these vanes with additional paint that varies from the finish description in this guide. Also, pivot wear can be reproduced at any time.*

# II. Brassware and Tinware

## Contents

Overall Height: 11"
Spout to Handle Width: 20 $^7/_8$"
Base Diameter: 6 $^5/_{16}$"

# Tin Gooseneck Coffee Pot                 29

New England auctions and sales reports have given written testimony to the successful deception of the fake coffee pot that you see illustrated here. Dealers and collectors throughout that area, accepting this pot as real, have paid well over $1000 a copy for it. It is, without question, one of the best fakes I have ever seen.

The aged tin-like material, punched decorations and attention paid to detail have made a "Fabulous Fake" that is extremely hard to identify. Collectors would be well advised to have access to one of these for comparison purposes.

Interior decorators will find in this aged replication a marvelous highlight for an early American room setting.

Construction: The coffee pot is essentially made in two halves. There is a seam running from top to bottom under the handle and one from just under the top ring, running down to the bottom of the pot through the spout. It is fabricated from .022" thick sheet steel with crimped and soldered seams.

The top edge of the pot, the edges of the handle and the bottom edge are roll-formed over wires. The handle wire serves as the pot lid hinge. The top edge of the pot is part of a roll-formed ring that serves as the final assembly piece for the body of the pot.

The pot lid is topped with a little mushroom shaped brass knob soldered in place. Another interesting construction detail is the flat area on the underside of the gooseneck spout. This is the result of the forming process used on the upper portion of the spout.

A large parrot beaked bird dominates the punched decoration on the side of the coffeepot. Garlands and stylized flowers complete the pattern. The punching is done on the outside surface of the pot with a flat bottom punch prior to the component forming and assembly.

Finish: The sheet steel used in the manufacture of this pot is given a lightly corroded finish. A final light staining wax coating is used to stabilize the finish and prevent further rusting. You have to see this finish to believe it. It is great!

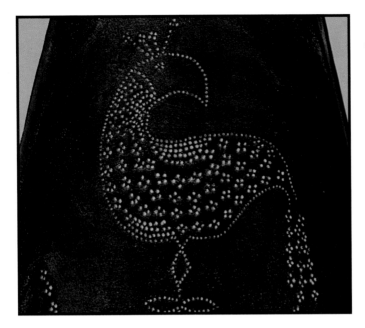

*The wonderful folksy detail presented here is typical for both sides of the coffee pot.*

**Fake Tip-offs**

Tinware of this quality is very difficult to identify as a fake. However there are several things that have been overlooked by the manufacturer.

**1.** The brass knob on top of the coffee pot lid is a fake design, created for this pot only. A brass roll pin and a brass plain flat washer are brazed together. The open end of the roll pin is pushed through the washer and filled with brass brazing material, then formed, ground and polished to finished size. The roll pin can easily be identified by its vertical seam on the knob shank.

**2.** The bird and flower design punched on the sides of the coffee pot is done with the punch indentations and a raised pattern on the inside of the pot. On most authentic antiques, the punched design creates a raised pattern on the outside of the object.

**3.** On the bottom of an antique coffee pot there would be evidence of wear due to normal use in a household. The fake coffee pot has none of this wear when it first comes from the manufacturer. However, watch out for the addition of simulated wear.

# Tin Document Box 30

In colonial America, the safekeeping of documents was important. Living conditions then were much different. Household pests, such as mice and bugs, made the storage of paper difficult. The tin document box was a solution to this problem. The first boxes were plain tin, but as time passed they evolved into the painted form.

Construction: This document box is fabricated from .022" thick sheet steel in a bent tab and soldered seam assembly. The cover, hand-formed in a dome shape, has its bottom edge roll-formed over pieces of wire to form a smooth round edge that facilitates closing. The upper edge is formed the same way. The ring handle on the cover, made from 1/8" steel rod, is held in place with a soldered sheet steel strap.

Finish: The paint finish is applied directly over the mill-supplied material surface.

**Fake Tip-offs**

**1.** Most authentic antique document boxes have been fabricated from .012" thick sheet.

**2.** Japanning, a technique used on antique document boxes, coated them with a translucent black varnish. It was not used on this fake. Black enamel has been used instead.

**3.** On old tin boxes, wear occurs around the edge of the bottom. Japanning generally remains in the center of the bottom because its surface is concave. The wear appears as a softly worn, almost polished, condition, with no heavy scratches or marks. There is no wear on the bottom of this fake.

**Height: 5 1/4"**
**Length: 6"**
**Width: 3 13/16"**

# Tin Document Box                    31

You are looking at a larger fake version of an American tin document box. Its brightly painted exterior displays a cheerful colonial charm.

Construction: This box, fabricated from .022" thick sheet steel, uses a bent tab and soldered seam assembly method. The cover, hand-formed in a dome shape, has its bottom edge rolled over pieces of wire to form a smooth round surface that eases closing. The upper part of the box has its edge formed the same way. The ring handle, formed out of 1/8" steel rod, is held in place by a sheet steel strap, soldered to the top of the cover.

Finish: The colorful paint finish is applied directly over the mill-supplied material surface.

**Fake Tip-off**

For the fake tip-offs that apply to this document box, see data sheet #30.

**Height: 5 $^7/_8$"**
**Length: 10 $^1/_8$"**
**Width: 3 $^7/_8$"**

# Brass Barber's Bowls

**Overall Diameter:**
**Large Bowl, 8 $^1/_{16}$"   Small Bowl, 6"**
**Depth: 1 $^1/_2$", Large and Small**

For eighteenth century barbers, straight razors, soap lather and surgery were the order of the day. One of the accessories used was a bowl designed to fit against the human form.

Construction: Sheet brass cut to a predetermined form is then hand hammered into shape. The bowl edges are rolled over copper wire and hammered closed. Brass tabs and hanging rings are riveted on the edge using copper rivets.

Finish: The brass surface is polished, but with restraint. Hand tooling marks and other imperfections are not removed.

**Fake Tip-off**
After use these bowls probably were hung on wall hooks. This action would have resulted in substantial wear on the inside of the hanging ring. Also the outer edge of the bowl's lip would have been worn from contact with the wall. There is no evidence of wear on the fakes.

# Tin Candle Box  **33**

In order to gain a measure of protection against pests, tin boxes were made to store candles. Protection was afforded not only by the tin construction but also by hanging the box in an inaccessible location.

The candle box illustrated here is a replica of a nineteenth-century design. Its aged looking, rusted tin construction is complete with a cracked and weathered paint finish. It is a superb "Fabulous Fake" and a way to add a colonial domestic touch to your home without the cost of an original antique.

**Overall Height: 8"**          **Overall Length: 11 1/4"**          **Body Diameter: 4 1/2"**

Construction: Sheet steel, .022" thick, is cut to size and roll-formed to shape. Crimped and soldered seams are used to accomplish the box assembly. The edges of the cover and back piece are roll-formed over wire, creating smooth, round edges. The box opening is 3 1/8" wide x 7 5/8" long. The wire in the box cover serves as the hinge for the cover catch. Two wire loops, fastened to the back with tabs of sheet steel, are soldered in place.

Finish: The entire box is prime coated and finished with a green paint. Prior to the painting, the tin material is given a corrosive treatment for the specific purpose of creating a rusted surface that looks authentic, especially when some of the painted finish has chipped off.

## Fake Tip-offs

**1.** Sheet tin that was used in colonial times was in the range of .012". The material used in the construction of this fake is almost twice that thickness.

**2.** The heavy primer coat applied to the fake boxes is a practice that is a trademark of modern manufacturers. Authentic antiques use none of this heavy primer.

**3.** Antique candle boxes exhibit considerable wear on their back surfaces, made from contact with walls during use. The hanging rings generally are mis-shapen and show signs of wear. All this is missing on the fakes.

*Cracked and chipped paint strengthens the illusion of age.*

# Tin Candle Box

Another nineteenth-century-looking candle box, this is similar to the green one illustrated on data sheet #33. Like other fakes, it captures the feeling of a real antique.

Construction: Sheet steel .022" thick is sized and roll-formed to shape. Assembly is accomplished using crimped and soldered seams. The edges of the cover and back piece are roll-formed over wire to make smooth round edges. The box opening is 3 1/8" wide by 7 5/8" long. The wire in the box cover serves as the hinge for the cover catch. Two wire loops, fastened to the back, are soldered in place with tabs of sheet steel.

Finish: A corrosive process is used to prematurely age its surface. A red primer, a finish coat of red paint, a few chips, a little rust and there you have it... a tin candle box that looks 200 years old.

## Fake Tip-offs

**1.** Authentic antique boxes used tin sheet .012" thick. This fake has used sheet almost twice that size.

**2.** A heavy red primer coat was only used on fake boxes.

**3.** There is no evidence of normal wear on the back or hanging rings of the fake box.

**Overall Height: 8"**
**Overall Length: 11 1/4"**
**Body Diameter: 4 1/2"**

# Tin Barber's Bowl    **35**

Bright red paint and a deep top hat configuration mark this barber's bowl as a probable American style. Its delightful nineteenth-century paint decoration and aged finish have created an item that could pass as authentically old.

Construction: Sheet steel has been cut to size and roll-formed to shape. Plain soldered overlapping seams fasten the assembly together. The half moon cutout and the rim of the bowl have their edges roll-formed over wire, resulting in smooth round edges. The bowl's bottom panel is dish-formed and has been soldered in place.

Finish: The steel material used in this fabrication has been corrosively treated. The mildly rusted finish resulting from this is painted with a top coat of red paint. Hand painted flowers decorate both sides of the bowl cutout and the bottom panel. Colors and decorations vary throughout the range of sizes.

## Fake Tip-off

The paint, while looking old, does not have the wear that would be consistent with a piece almost two hundred years old. There should be signs of wear on the top edge of the wide rim and on the bottom outside edge of the bowl. There is no sign of wear on this fake.

**Sizes range up to the following:**
**Overall Diameter: 11"**
**Base Diameter: 4 3/8"**
**Height: 4 1/2"**

# Tin Tea Canisters                    36

Bright colors with gold and black highlight these tins that were originally used to ship and store oriental teas. Still made in the same section of the world, these fakes possess many of the original's qualities and they are sure to make a dramatic statement in today's interiors.

Construction: A mild sheet steel is cut to the proper size and roll formed. The steel pieces are assembled with crimped seams that are permanently fastened together with solder.

Finish: The canister is corrosively treated to give it a slightly rusted surface. A cracked primer coat and a color finish are applied to its exterior. The gold and black labeling on the front side completes the painting process. A staining wax applied over the dried paint highlights the primer cracks and effectively ages the surface.

**Fake Tip-offs**

**1.** Cracked primer with a color finish coat over it is an aging process used on fake canisters only. On authentic antiques the finish coat of color would be cracked. The heavy red and brown primers are used only on fakes.

**2.** The gilt labels on the front of the fake canisters do not exhibit any signs of age. Old labels would be crazed with small age cracks and show definite signs of wear.

**3.** The bottom of the canister and the bottom edge of the canister cap should show considerable wear. They would have abraded and worn spots where contact was made. The fake canisters do not have this wear.

**Overall Height; 17 $^3/_8$"**
**Base Diameter: 9 $^1/_8$"**
**Top Cover Diameter: 5"**

# Brassware and Tinware Summary

The fake tip-offs described at the end of each data sheet outline the most obvious features that label each a fake. There are other things that can be used to help in your determination of an item's age. They are the subtle differences that you would perhaps not notice unless they were pointed out.

Sheet brass items are relatively easy to fake. Brass does not easily corrode, therefore a polished surface would be considered a normal condition for a truly old piece. However, when examined with a magnifying glass, an old brass surface will show a criss-crossing pattern of minute scratches. It is these scratches that give old brass that special soft look. New brass lacks this pattern of scratches and, under a glass, may exhibit the one directional scratches of the rolling mill that made the sheet.

Tinware also has a characteristic of age that is hard to fake. Authentically old sheet tin was an iron core with a layer of pure tin on each side. As pieces aged with use and corrosion, this sandwich of metal would deteriorate in a predictable way. Exterior surfaces exposed to ambient conditions would turn a soft brownish grey, with rust showing as a few small freckles. Interior surfaces would have retained most of their shiny tin coating, with rust showing as occasional boils or spots. The fake tinware has been made from thin sheet steel and has had no tin coating. It just rusts.

If you are able to keep all of these things in mind when passing judgment on a questionable piece, you should have no trouble in identifying fakes.

# III. Tin Candle Sconces

## Contents

# Round Reflector, Single Sconce 37

The round reflector back on this sconce has been tooled to simulate a more expensive mirrored construction. An original of this style is pictured in the Early Lighting Guide of the Rushlight Club, an American organization.

Construction: The outer rim of the round reflector is rolled over a piece of wire, adding strength and creating a smooth edge. Smooth rolled annular beads, with an offset radial segment pattern, are formed in the reflector from the front side. A curved bracket with rolled edges attaches the candle tray to the reflector. Soldered construction and an inner bracing arm across the bracket make the assembly strong. The 3 3/8" diameter candle tray has a crimped edge and provides a platform for a 7/8" diameter candle tube. The hanging hole that you see near the top edge of the reflector is 3/8" diameter and has the back side burr hammered flat around the edge of the hole.

Finish: The surface of this sconce has been mildly corroded and presents a relatively smooth surface. You will notice some minor rust, pitting and blistering.

**Reflector Diameter: 8 3/4"**
**Overall Height: 11 3/8"**
**Depth: 4"**

# Urn Shaped, Single Sconce

**38**

American colonial design is evident in this graceful urn shaped candle sconce. A country feeling is inspired with its double heart reflector pattern and fluted candle tray. It is hard to believe that this sconce is a fake.

**Overall Height; 14 ³/₈"**
**Width: 8 ¹/₈"**
**Depth: 4 ⁵/₈"**

Construction: Five pieces of .020" thick steel sheet are put together with bent tabs and solder fastening. The reflector back has its side and bottom edges rolled over pieces of wire to form smooth round edges. Two dimpled beads, 1 1/2" in from the reflector sides, run from the convex top curve to the candle tray bracket. The 1 3/16" wide candle tray bracket has been inserted through a slot cut in the reflector back, bent over and soldered in place. The 3 3/4 " diameter fluted tray holds a 7/8" diameter candle tube. The hanging hole at the top of the sconce reflector is 3/8" in diameter.

Finish: An antique look has been obtained by the use of a corrosive treatment.

### Handmade Construction

*In this closeup picture, you will notice that the formed grooves on the candle bracket have their outside edges bent back and hammered flat. Although it is not noticeable, the "S" bracket stiffener under the tray also has its outside edges bent back and hammered flat. The random pattern of fluting and irregular trimmed edge are signs of this handmade fabrication. This sconce has a natural steel mill finish with subtle indications of age. The corrosive pitting and light rusting of its special corrosive process are seen as the light brown areas on the candle tray.*

# Mirrored, Single Sconce          39

**Overall Height; 14 1/4"**
**Width: 4 1/2"**
**Depth:  3 3/16"**

A fluted top and square tray distinguish this fake sconce from the others. It has replicated features of early American design and construction. The distressed mirror, a rarely seen detail, has heightened the feeling of authentic age.

Construction: The metal portion of the sconce is made from eight pieces of .020" thick sheet steel. Tin or tinplate has not been used at all. Bent and soldered tabs are used to assemble the pieces. The sconce back has a shell-formed, rolled and crimped top edge, the irregular shape of which is caused by the hand forming and trimming process. The side edges, below the notches, are rolled over pieces of wire, creating a rounded edge on both sides. Two stiffening beads run from top to bottom on both sides of the mirror. The 8 3/4" by 2 5/8" mirror frame is made from formed sheet metal with mitred corners. The inner edge of the frame is bent back on itself and hammered flat. The base of the sconce is a 1 1/4" high square tray that holds a 7/8" diameter candle tube.

Finish: An antique look is achieved by the use of a corrosive treatment. It creates a superbly rusted surface that effectively hides the fact that steel is substituted for tin. Staining wax is used as a final finish to stabilize the rust and to add a centuries-old grime to its surface.

# Beaded, Single Sconce

The beaded edges on the back, tray and candle tube are distinctive features of this sconce. The tombstone shaped back and the punched flower decoration are of traditional design and American influence.

Construction: The sconce, made of four pieces of .020" thick sheet steel, has a bent and soldered tab construction. A 1/8" wide bead borders the edge of the tray and candle tube. A six-petal flower is prick punched into the back. The edges of the back are bent over 1/16" and hammered flat. The 1 1/4" high round tray takes a 7/8" diameter candle. A 3/8" diameter hanging hole is located approximately 1" down from the top edge of the sconce. The handmade character of this piece is most clearly evidenced by the random spacing and irregular pattern of the ribs in the beaded border.

**Overall Height; 14"**
**Width: 4 3/4"**
**Depth: 3 3/16"**

Finish: The sconce surface has been mildly corroded and presents a relatively smooth appearance with no evidence of heavy scaling. A secondary coating of staining wax is applied to retard further rusting, remove brown rust dust and add grime to the cracks and crevices of the sconce.

# Mirrored, Single Sconce

**Overall Height: 14 ³/8"**
**Width: 4 ¹/2"**
**Depth: 3"**

The round candle tray is the only difference between this single candle mirrored sconce and the one on the #39 data sheet. It also has early American design features and a construction similar to many of the sconces in this series.

Construction: Sheet steel, in place of tin or tinplate, .020" thick, is used for the metal details of this sconce. Its pieces are assembled using bent tabs and a soldered construction. The shell-formed back has a rolled and crimped top edge, the irregular shape of which has been caused by the hand forming and trimming process. The side edges, below the notches, are rolled over wires to create a round edge on both sides. Two stiffening beads run from top to bottom on both sides of the mirror. The 8 3/4" by 2 5/8" mirror frame, made from sheet metal, has mitred corners. The inner edge of the frame is bent back on itself and hammered flat. The base of the sconce is a 1 3/16" high round tray that holds a 7/8" diameter candle tube.

Finish: A corrosive treatment is used to effectively age the surface of the fake sconce with a film of rust. A final coating of staining wax is used to prevent further rusting and to add a bit of grime to the surface.

# Punched Heart, Single Sconce 42

This single candle sconce has an early American tin look that is tough to beat. The hand-punched decoration and the offset hanging tab are distinctive features of this fake lighting device.

Construction: Four pieces of .020" thick sheet steel with a bent tab and soldered construction are used in place of tin.

The back of this sconce, dramatically highlighted with an offset hanging tab, has the edge on either side of the tab, rolled over a piece of wire. The resulting round edge runs from the tab to the top of the candle tray on both sides. The decoration of the sconce is prick punched from the back. A single smooth running bead has been formed between the two rows of punch dimples on the back and around the top edge of the candle tray. The 1 3/16" high square tray holds a 7/8" diameter candle tube.

Finish: The surface of this sconce is mildly corroded. A staining wax finish has been applied to stabilize its aged appearance.

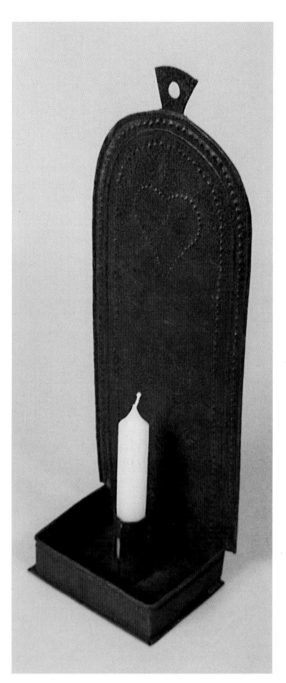

**Overall Height; 13 ³/₄"**
**Width: 5"**
**Depth: 3 ¹/₂"**

# Scalloped, Single Sconce

**Overall Height; 13"**
**Width: 5 3/8"**
**Depth: 3 1/4"**

Because it is manufactured from a heavier material than most, this fake sconce is a natural for electrification. The additional strength has created the stable platform necessary for the stress of wiring and its maintenance.

Construction: The sheet metal assembly consists of eight pieces of .030" thick steel put together with bent tabs and solder fastening. The sconce has its top edge rolled over, crimped and then bent back parallel with the front surface. A single formed bead runs across the top, along with two beads running down each side. Both side edges are rolled over fine rods or pieces of wire to create round, smooth edges.
The 2 1/4" by 7 7/8" mirror is held in place by a mitred steel frame. The inner edge of the frame is bent back on itself and hammered flat. A rectangular, 1 3/16" high tray, holding a 7/8" diameter candle tube, forms the base of the sconce.

Finish: A corrosive treatment is used to create the illusion of age. The rusting and pitting created by this process are stabilized with a final top coat of light green primer.

# Beaded Edge, Single Sconce     44

The construction of this fake sconce is the same as the one on data sheet #40. The only difference between the two is the shape of the candle tray. The shape of #40 is round and this one is rectangular.

Construction: The sconce is made of four pieces of .020" sheet steel with a bent and soldered tab construction. A 3/16" wide bead borders the back of the sconce. A 1/8" bead borders the edge of the tray and candle tube. You will notice that the seam of the candle tube is positioned towards the front edge of the tray. A six-petal flower is prick punched into the back side of the reflector. The edges of the back are bent over 1/16" and hammered flat. The 1 1/4" high rectangular candle tray holds a 7/8" diameter candle tube. A 3/8" diameter hanging hole is located approximately 1" down from the top edge of the sconce. The entire sconce is made by hand, evidenced by the random spacing and irregular patterns of its decorative elements.

Finish: The corrosive finishing process that the sconce receives is remarkable. It adds two hundred years of age to its appearance, almost overnight. The process has been used as described on data sheet #40.

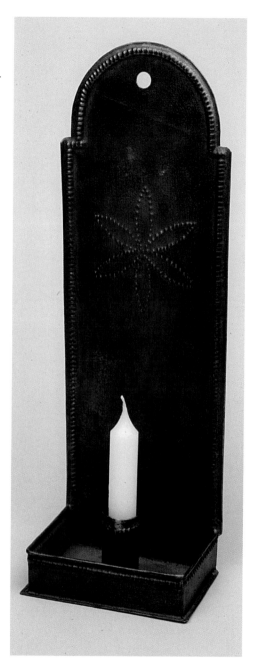

**Overall Height; 13"**
**Width: 5 3/8"**
**Depth: 3 1/4"**

# Mirrored Scalloped, Single Sconce    45

**Overall Height; 13"**
**Width: 5 3/8"**
**Depth: 3 1/4"**

The fake sconce shown on data sheet #43 has a rectangular candle tray. It is basically the same as the sconce pictured here except for the tray design. A heavier steel material has been substituted for the lightweight tin of authentic antiques. The added strength of material has made a stable platform of the sconce, so very necessary for the stress of modern wiring.

Construction: The sheet metal assembly consists of eight pieces of .030" thick steel put together with bent tabs and solder fastening. The sconce back has the top edge rolled over, crimped and then bent back parallel with the front surface. A single formed bead runs across the top, along with two beads running down each side. Both side edges are rolled over fine rods or pieces of wire to create round, smooth edges.

The 2 1/4" by 7 7/8" mirror is held in place by a mitred steel frame. The inner edge of the frame is bent back on itself and hammered flat. A 1 3/16" high tray, holding a 7/8" diameter candle tube, forms the base of the sconce.

Finish: A corrosive process is used to create the illusion of age. The rust and pitting of this process are stabilized with a light green primer coat of paint.

# Mirrored Scalloped, Single Sconce

# 46

This sconce has a good eighteenth-century look. The aged mirror and corroded surface of the metal are the ultimate in faux finishes. It is usable as a source of light and is historically accurate.

Construction: The sheet metal assembly consists of eight pieces of .020" thick steel put together with bent tabs and solder fastening. The sconce back has the top edge rolled over, crimped and then bent back parallel with the front surface. A single formed bead runs across the top, along with two beads running down each side. Both side edges are rolled over pieces of wire to create round, smooth edges. The 2 7/16" x 8" mirror is held in place by a mitred steel frame. The inner edge of the frame is bent back on itself and hammered flat. A round 1 1/8" high tray, holding a 1" diameter candle tube, forms the base of the sconce.

Finish: The entire steel portion of the sconce has been given a corrosive treatment to obtain the aged look of an eighteenth-century antique. A wonderful rusted finish results from this process. The mirror has also been creatively aged. After the aging process, a final coat of staining wax is applied to stabilize the finish and to prevent further rusting.

**Overall Height; 12 7/8"**
**Width: 5 3/16"**
**Depth: 3"**

# Punched Flower, Double Sconce 47

**Overall Height; 16 5/8"**
**Width: 6 1/8"**
**Depth: 3 11/16"**

The simple elegance of colonial tin has been created in this fake by its punched flower decoration and fluted top. However, the double candle design, while aesthetically fine, does not appear to be an authentic copy of a true antique. It is rather the expansion of a single candle design by the fake manufacturer in an effort to increase his product line. Its aged finish has made this sconce almost believable as an antique.

Construction: This sconce is made from five pieces of .020" thick mild steel sheet using bent tabs and solder. The top of the sconce back has a shell-formed, rolled and crimped top edge. Both sides of the sconce back are rolled over pieces of wire, creating smooth rounded edges. There are three stiffening beads running down each side of the sconce back. A simple six-petal flower is hand punched into the back, nine inches up from the bottom. The 1 3/8" high rectangular candle tray holds two 1" diameter candle tubes, fastened in place with tabs soldered to the bottom of the tray. Located three inches down from the top edge of the sconce is a 3/8" diameter hanging hole. It is punched through from the front resulting in a rough metal burr on the back side that is flattened around the hole edge.

Finish: The entire sconce is given a corrosive treatment that has delightfully rusted its metal surface. A final coat of staining wax is used to stabilize the rust and to add a little grime.

# Mirrored Scalloped, Double Sconce    48

This sconce may not represent an authentic copy of an antique; however, it has a rather naive appearance that works well in a country decorating scheme.

Construction: Made of nine pieces of .020" sheet steel, this sconce has a bent and soldered tab construction. The back has the top edge rolled over, crimped and then bent back parallel with the front surface. A single hand-formed bead runs across the top of the mirror with three beads running down each side. Both sides are rolled over fine rods or pieces of wire creating smooth round edges. The 3" by 8" aged mirror is held in place with a mitred steel frame. The inner edge of the frame is bent back on itself and hammered flat. A rounded 1 1/8" high tray holding two 1" diameter candle tubes forms the base of the sconce.

Finish: The sconce, with its irregular decorative patterns and crude workmanship, has been given a corrosive aging treatment that has effectively removed most traces of its modern manufacture. A top coat of staining wax has added grime to its surface.

**Overall Height; 16 3/4"**
**Width: 7 1/2"**
**Depth: 4"**

**Overall Height; 16 ³/₄"**
**Width: 6 ³/₁₆"**
**Depth: 3 ¹⁵/₁₆"**

Great age and the appearance of a hard life are characteristics of this two candle fake sconce. Heavy corrosion and scaling combined with two repairs in the back give it an old look. Don't let the illusion of age fool you. This is a modern version of a single candle sconce.

Construction: Made of nine pieces of .017" thick sheet steel, it has a bent and soldered tab construction. The top of the sconce back has a shell-formed, rolled and crimped top edge. Both sides of the sconce, below the notches, are rolled over pieces of wire creating smooth, rounded edges. The 2 9/16" by 8 1/2" aged mirror is held in place with a mitre-formed tin frame. The frame has the inner edge bent back on itself and hammered flat. There are three stiffening beads running down each side of the mirror. The 1 5/8" high rounded candle tray holds two 7/8" diameter candle tubes.

Finish: The sconce surface is heavily rusted with a corrosive treatment. The two repairs to the back are evidence of the corrosive process burning through the metal. A staining wax coating is the final manufacturing process.

# Scalloped Tray, Triple Sconce 50

Three candles make this sconce interesting but not historically accurate. I doubt that this design ever existed as an authentic antique. It was more than likely the marketing ambition of the fake manufacturer that created it.

Construction: The sconce back has the top edge rolled over, crimped and then bent back parallel with the front surface. A single bead is formed across the top, with four beads running down both sides. Both sides are rolled over fine wire, creating round edges. The 4 3/8" by 9 7/16" mirror is framed with a mitred sheet metal frame. The inner edge of the frame is bent back on itself and hammered flat. A scalloped 1 5/16" high tray holding three 7/8" diameter candle tubes forms the base of the sconce.

Finish: The eighteenth-century-style construction has its modern birth disguised by the use of a corrosive aging treatment. The resulting rusted surface is stabilized with a final coating of staining wax that has also added a bit of ancient-looking grime.

**Overall Height; 19 1/8"**
**Width: 9 3/4"**
**Depth: 5"**

# Mirrored, Triple Sconce 51

**Overall Height; 18 3/4"**
**Width: 8 1/2"**
**Depth: 4 5/8"**

Although some of the design features of this sconce are eighteenth century, the three candle size probably never existed as an authentic antique. The skill of the fake manufacturer has effectively masked the tool marks of modern machining with a superb surface treatment. The sconce looks antique.

Construction: Made of ten pieces of .020" sheet steel with a bent and soldered tab construction, it makes a sizable lighting device. The top of the sconce back has a shell-formed, rolled and crimped top edge. Both sides of the sconce, below the notches, are rolled over pieces of wire, forming smooth rounded edges. The 1 1/2" by 9 1/2" aged mirror is held in place by a formed sheet metal frame. The mitred frame has the inner edge bent back on itself and hammered flat. There are four stiffening beads running down each side of the mirror. The 1 1/4" high rectangular candle tray holds three 7/8" diameter candle tubes.

Finish: The sconce surface has been rapidly oxidized with a special treatment. You will notice on the upper right hand side of the back an attempted repair to a small hole. This will occur on many of the sconces. Corroded holes and their crude repairs reinforce the "period" feeling of these sconces. A wax final coating completes the manufacturing process.

### Simulated Age

*You are looking at the front of the sconce. The small burn hole is shown with an attempted solder repair. The brown speckled appearance of the sheet metal surface is actually corrosion pitting, part of the process that caused the burn hole. I must point out that the corrosive aging is not a precise process, and the results can vary from the mild condition that you see here to a very heavy scaling.*

# Mirrored, Triple Sconce

**Overall Height; 18 3/8"**
**Width: 8 3/8"**
**Depth: 5 1/4"**

It is doubtful that a sconce of this design ever existed as a real antique. Multiple candle sconces were not often seen. This one certainly looks like a related version of the single sconce shown on data sheet #40. In spite of its dubious design origin, this fake sconce could pass in many circles as a true colonial American lighting device.

Construction: Because sheet tin or tinplate was not readily available, mild low carbon steel has been used in its place. Ten pieces of steel sheet, .020" thick, are assembled with bent tabs and solder. The top of the sconce back has a shell-formed, rolled and crimped top edge. Both sides of the sconce below the notches are rolled over pieces of fine wire to form smooth round edges. The 4 1/2"by 9 1/2" aged mirror is held in place by a formed sheet steel frame. The mitred frame has the inner edge bent back on itself and hammered flat. There are four stiffening beads that run down each side of the mirror. The 1 1/8" high round candle tray hold three 1" diameter candle tubes.

Finish: The sconce is aged with a corrosive treatment that leaves a film of rust on all of its steel surfaces. With the aged mirror in place, a final coat of staining wax is used to stabilize the rust.

# Tin Sconce Summary & Fake Tip-offs

True remnants of American colonial lighting are scarce. Tin candle sconces, because of their fragile construction and their susceptability to corrosion, are one of the forms least likely to have survived. Yet we find thousands of these in today's antiques shows and flea markets. Why?

They are plentiful because they are fakes. They are cheap and easy to make with a very high profit return on investment. Only basic sheet metal hand tools are required to manufacture them.

The fakes illustrated in this guide are very good quality and handmade. Each has its own individual characteristics. Dimensions and detail construction can and often will vary between sconces. Even the corrosively aged finishes vary from lot to lot. You will find sconces have finish variants from mild surface film rust to surface pitting and heavy scaling rust.

## Beware of Fraud

The individual nature of these sconces has caused confusion among the antique buying public. I stood next to a person examining a broken mirrored sconce being offered for sale at a Brimfield, Massachusetts, flea market. It was a broken fake being examined. I listened in amazement as the dealer explained away its broken condition. He said that the sconce was an unfinished original antique and was a rare find. His pitch hit home, for the unsuspecting person bought it, to the tune of $300. The dealer was a real con artist, for on his table of wares for sale were other fake lighting devices. Had this person been able to check his find against known fakes, the fraud would have been seen and the loss of $300 avoided.

If you are going to be buying antique or fake sconces, be an informed buyer. Read the information in this chapter and study the **Fake Tip-offs** that follow. They will save you a lot of money.

### Fake Tip-offs

**1.** The single candle form of sconce illustrated in this chapter is quite likely to be historically correct. I doubt the authenticity of the double candle design and the triple candle design is definitely a creation of the fakers. There are very few real antique multiple candle sconces. It looks like the fake manufacturer simply expanded his product line of single candle sconces to include double and triple versions.

**2.** All of the sconces in this chapter have been fabricated from sheet steel. The sheet iron (tin) or tinplate of original antiques was either too expensive or was not available to the fake manufacturer. One of the ways to tell which material has been used is to examine the finish. All of the sconces in this section have been artificially aged. Rust on tinplate is evidenced by occasional spots that burn through or pit the surface. Most of the metal will present an even thin rust film, not the heavy scaling or pitting that covers most of the fakes. Be immediately suspicious of any sconce with heavy corrosion.

**3.** All the fake sconces shown in this chapter have been made by the same manufacturer. They all have a 3/8" diameter hole located at the top of the reflector back. It is a perfectly round hole with no evidence of wear. Also there is no wear to be seen on the back of the reflector where the metal would come in contact with the wall. Real antiques should have some indication of wear.

# IV. Lighting Devices

## Contents

(con't)

(con't)

**Overall Height; 20 ³/₄"**
**(to top of ring)**
**Shade Diameter: 6 ⁵/₈"**
**Base Diameter: 7 ¹/₄"**

# Tin Student Two Candle Lamp        **53**

The elegance of an early nineteenth-century drawing room can be imagined as the setting for this student candle lamp. Recreated faithfully from an original English design, it is as functional today as it was then.

The two candle holders are adjustable up or down and are locked in position by a center thumb screw. The shades are also easily adjustable and can be locked in place with a thumb screw.

Stability, a quality that is so important in a lighting device of any sort, is suitably provided by a heavily weighted tin base.

Construction: The center shaft and the top finial with ring are fabricated from brass. The rest of the lamp is made from steel sheet. Riveting, soldering and crimping are fastening methods used on this assembly. The lamp base is filled with sand and soldered closed.

Finish: The lamp has a red and gold finish. A green and gold combination is also available. The center shaft is left with a natural brass finish and the two shades are painted white on the inside.

## Fake Tip-offs

**1.** There is an almost complete lack of wear on the brass center shaft. The shades and candle holders are adjustable and would have produced some sort of scuffing on the center shaft had the light really been old.

**2.** The bottom surface of the weighted base on a well-used antique would have the smooth fuzzy marks of wear on its high spots. The faker of the lamp did not add wear to its base, leaving it definitely tagged as new. Be careful. It is not out of the question for an unscrupulous antique dealer to add simulated wear to that surface. Most of that wear would be coarse scratching compared to the fine abrasion caused by years of actual use.

**3**. The sheet metal parts exhibit no deterioration of their painted surfaces. The paint, slightly faded by design, has no age cracking or peeling, and corrosion is nonexistent. The painted surface on an antique lighting device of this type would certainly show its age.

# Angel Candelabra

# 54

Nineteenth-century European holiday tradition may have influenced the designers of this folksy angel candelabra. Although whimsical in character, it provides for the mounting of three candles in metal sconces for use as a light source.

**Overall Height; 15"**
**Maximum Width: 7 1/2"**
**Base Diameter: 3 1/2"**

Construction: The angel is carved from soft wood similar to tropical balsa. Its sheet steel wings are bonded to the back of the upper torso. The three candle sconces are made from sheet steel as a soldered assembly. Two of these have rods angled out from their lower cones and soldered in place. They are held in place by the angel's hands and have been tightly pressed into holes in its body. The third candle holder has no lower cone but rather a rod soldered in place that has been pressed into a hole in the angel's head.

Finish: The metal pieces are lightly corroded. The wooden parts are brightly painted with enough intentional abrasion to give it a feeling of age.

## Fake Tip-off

Because of its light wood construction, it is prone to tipping over. A European antique would have used locally available heavy wood for its construction.

# Round Chamber Candle Holder          55

The shimmering images in the pan of the chamber holder are a reflection of its handmade quality. Its hammered brass construction is typical of eighteenth-century methods. The long handle and copper rivet fastening are features of its European design.

Construction: The holder pan, formed from one piece of heavy brass sheet, has its bottom surface concave to allow proper clearance for the candle tube fastening rivets. The 5/8" high pan edge has a 3/32" thick sheet brass handle copper riveted to one of the sides. A 7/16" diameter hanging hole is located at the outer end of the handle. In the center of the pan two copper rivets hold the candle tube in place.

**Pan Diameter: 5 $^3/_4$"**
**Handle Length: 5 $^3/_4$"**

Finish: All the surfaces and edges are highly polished. The polishing has effectively removed all the sharp edges and blended the tool marks into the finished surface.

## Fake Tip-off

On authentically old brass pieces, wear is characterized by many minute scratches that form a dull, fuzzy-looking surface. The metal actually gets worn away by abrasion. This surface texture is missing on this fake lighting device.

# Oval Chamber Candle Holder 56

This candle holder is similar to the one on data sheet #55. The distinguishing feature of this holder is its oval shape. Its brass material has been hand-crafted using traditional eighteenth-century European methods and design.

**Overall Width: 6 1/8"**
**Overall Length; 10 1/4"**

Construction: Hand -formed from sheet brass, its bottom surface has been concave shaped to allow clearance for the candle tube fastening rivet heads. The 5/8" high pan edge has the holder handle riveted to the middle of one of its oval long sides. The 7/16" diameter hanging hole is located at the outer end of the handle. In the center of the pan, two rivets are used to hold the candle tube in place.

Finish: All the surfaces and edges are highly polished. This polishing has effectively removed all the sharp edges and blended all of the tool marks into the finish.

**Fake Tip-off**

On naturally old brass pieces, wear is characterized by many minute scratches that form a dull, fuzzy-looking surface. The metal actually gets worn away by abrasion. This surface texture is missing on this fake lighting device.

# Adjustable Pendant, One Candle 57

The candle adjustment of this lighting device is obtained by adjusting the saw tooth trammel. Also, this design has a dual use. It not only holds candles, but the pivoting candle holder arm serves double duty as a rush holder. Another interesting feature is a candle push-up, seen protruding from the bottom of the candle socket.

This somewhat delicate looking lighting device had its origin in the weaving industry and became known under the general term of loom light. It was used as a light source during weaving operations and hung from the weaving looms themselves, to get the light closer to the work.

It is an attractive device with many hand-forged and moving parts. Certainly usable today as a candle holder, it could be an excellent source of accent light in a historical setting. With its great re-creation of an aged finish, you would be hard pressed to tell the difference between this "Fabulous Fake" and the original loom light.

Construction: The saw tooth form of the trammel is cut from 3/32" thick sheet steel. At the top of this saw tooth is a sheet steel retainer welded in place. The bottom has a forged offset for the hinge point of the candle arm.

The steel fabricated hanger rod has its top end terminated in a welded swivel hanger. The other end of the hanger rod has a closed eye that holds the saw tooth adjustment loop. The candle arm is a combination welded and forged assembly. Its offset forged hinge joint has a steel rivet hinge pin. The commonality of the material used is evidenced by the candle push-up being fabricated from the same square bar as the hanger rod.

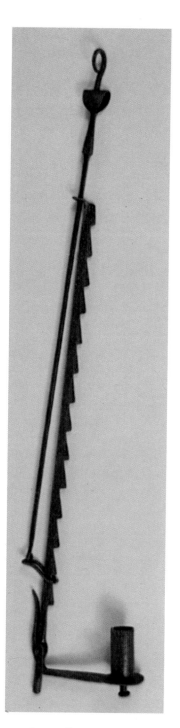

**Overall Length;**
**43 1/4" maximum**
**27 3/8" minimum**

Finish: A corrosive treatment is used to condition the surface of the entire adjustable pendant candle holder. Its modern steel mill finish has been changed to the rust and pitting of a centuries old antique. A staining wax final coating is sometimes used to stabilize the finish and prevent further rusting.

## Fake Tip-offs

**1.** Look closely at the candle tube fastening to the arm. On this fake, twentieth-century electric or gas welding has been used to fasten the tube to the arm. An authentically old loom light would have been hand-forged, a process that did not add metal to the joint. You will find this to be true of all the weld joints on this lighting device.

**2.** Examine the inside of the hanging loop and the two adjustment loops. There is almost a complete lack of noticeable wear on their surfaces. A real antique would show some signs of wear on these surfaces.

# Adjustable Pendant, Two Candle

This is another version of an old loom light. A single candle version of this is shown on data sheet #57. It has the same operational characteristics as the single candle holder. It is adjusted vertically by moving the hanger rod to a new saw tooth setting and lateral adjustment is obtained by swiveling at the top of the pendant.

Construction: The trammel fabrication is identical to the single candle version. The primary construction differences are from the pivot to and including the double candle holder. The candle holder drip pan is made from flat sheet steel with a small lip around the edge. The pan measures 3 3/16" wide by 6 3/4" long. Two formed sheet steel candle tubes, equally spaced on the top surface of the drip pan, are welded in place. The dual candle holder's overall depth is 7 5/8".

Finish: The entire adjustable pendant candle is given a corrosive that has produced a great aged finish. Centuries of age are reproduced. A final finish of staining wax is used to prevent further rusting.

**Fake Tip-offs**

**1.** The candle tubes are fastened to the arm using twentieth-century gas or electric welding. An antique loom light would have been hand forged, a process that did not add metal to the joint. There are no forge welded joints on this fake pendant! Only modern welding has been used.

**Overall Length;
43" maximum
26 3/8" minimum**

**2.** The hanging loop and the two adjustment loops show no wear on their surfaces. An antique piece would show appreciable wear on these surfaces.

# Adjustable Pendant Pan Lamp 59

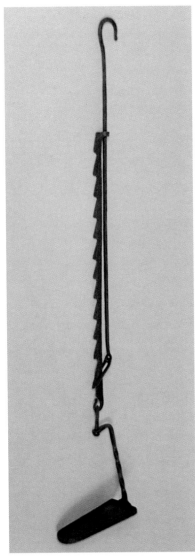

**Pan Length; 6"**
**Pan Width: 2 ⁵/₈"**
**Overall Length:**
**45 ¹/₂" max.**
**32" min.**

Pan lamps represent one of the earliest forms of primitive lighting. The saw tooth trammel of this one provides the vertical adjustment, while its swivel eye allows positioning of the pan.

Construction: The vertical hanger, formed from 1/4" diameter steel rod, has its upper end terminated in a forged hook and its lower end in an eye. The steel saw tooth part of the trammel is assembled at the lower end by an elongated hanger loop that engages the teeth. The upper end of the saw tooth piece is retained by a welded loop that captures the hanger rod. The saw tooth steel frame has tapered teeth for ease of trammel adjustment. On a real antique they would be forge tapered. On this fake they are ground to that shape using an electric grinder. The lower end of the saw tooth frame is forged into a captivating loop for the lamp swivel eye. It would not surprise me to find that the swivel eye is made from a common nail with the head welded and the tail tapered into a loop.

The pan lamp construction is more conventional. Sheet steel forms the base and sides of the lamp. The corners are welded, finish ground and treated to resemble hand-forged iron. A hanger arm riveted to the back side of the pan finishes the assembly.

Finish: The entire surface of this lighting device has received a corrosive treatment to develop the rust-pitted finish that you see in the illustration. A final finish of staining wax may be used to stabilize the surface and prevent further rusting.

## Fake Tip-offs

**1.** The pan lamp corners are electrically welded using twentieth-century equipment. A small amount of weld burn-through can be seen on the inside of the corners.

**2.** On the inside of the top hanging hook, the adjustment loop and the lamp swivel loops, there should be a substantial amount of wear on a real antique. This fake has no wear.

*The sawtooth trammel is shown 90 degrees out of its true hanging position.*

# Loom Light

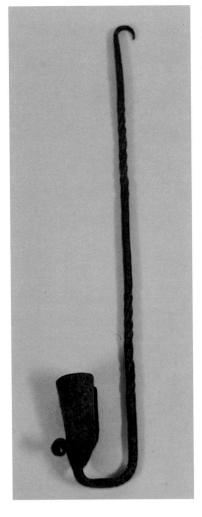

**Overall Height;
15 ¹/₂"**

Originally hand-forged from one piece of iron bar, this fake version of a loom light is one of the simplest forms ever used by the weaving industry. It exhibits design details that you do not often find on a device this simple. An interesting, slightly twisted shaft and a little curl on the front of the candle socket are two. They are gentle reminders of the eighteenth-century craftsmen that first produced this design.

Construction: The vertical shaft is fabricated from 3/16" square steel bar. Two twisted sections alternating with straight ones form the interesting design of the vertical shaft. A simple forged hook tops the shaft. The bottom of the shaft, bent almost at a right angle, is electrically welded to the formed steel candle socket. The steel curl is welded to the front of the candle socket. All the welds are ground with an electric grinder and treated to resemble hand-forged iron.

Finish: A corrosive treatment has rusted and pitted the light's surface, simulating centuries of use and wear. A staining wax is used to stabilize the surface and to prevent further rusting.

### Fake Tip-off

The welding used on the candle socket and decorative curl is twentieth-century technology. Look for signs of additional welding material in the joint. Indications of grinding may also be apparent.

# Adjustable Loom Light 61

A variant of the loom light on data sheet #60, this one allows adjustment of the candle height by the use of a trammel. It is a basic design, with the only decorative touch being the little curl of metal on the front of the candle socket.

Construction: A 5/32" by 1" steel strap, with the end forged into a hanging hook on the top and a right-angle retainer on the bottom for the candle holder arm, provides adjustment for this device. The candle holder arm, 5/16" in diameter and bent at the top ninety degrees, provides for candle adjustment when inserted in one of the holes in the hanging strap. The rolled candle tube is inserted in a slot at the end of the arm and crimped in place. A small curl of sheet steel, welded to the front of the candle holder, supplies a decorative touch.

**Overall Height;
22 1/4" maximum
14" minimum**

Finish: This fake, like the others in this chapter, has its aged appearance artificially created. A corrosive treatment has given its surface the rust and pitting of years of use. Staining wax occasionally is used to stabilize the finish and prevent further rusting.

**Fake Tip-off**

Look closely at the decorative curl. Modern welding material and grinding marks may be seen. Electric and gas welding are twentieth-century developments.

# Iron Chandelier, Three Candle 62

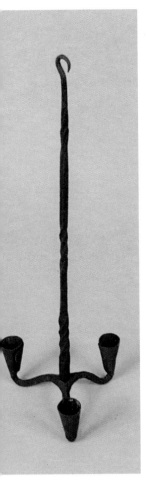

**Height; 18 ³/₄"**
**Diameter: 6 ⁵/₈"**

Three candle holders are presented in an unusual form with this device. The vertical shaft is divided into four round and three twisted sections, giving it character and interest.

Construction: The vertical shaft is a welded assembly, comprised of three sections of twisted square steel bar and four sections of round steel rod. The welds are finish ground, to blend with each shaft form, resulting in a hand-forged look. The shaft is topped with a forged hanging hook and the bottom terminated with a shoulder end.

The candle holder web is a welded assembly, fabricated from steel bar. The forged arms are tapered, arching out from the center to end in upturned slots. Formed sheet steel candle holders are inserted in the slots and welded in place. All the welds are finish ground and treated to resemble hand forging.

To assemble the shaft to the web, a hole is drilled in the web center. The shaft is inserted through the hole and tack-welded in place. A steel washer is then slipped over the protruding shaft end on the bottom of the web and welded in place.

Finish: A corrosive treatment that has rusted and pitted the metal surface eliminates most of the marks and indications of its modern manufacture. To stabilize the corrosion and to prevent further rusting, a final staining wax coating is sometimes applied.

## Fake Tip-offs

**1.** On the washer weld, located at the center of the web bottom, you will find indentations caused by ball-peen hammering. This has been done to disguise the weld and make it appear hand forged. These marks are not consistent with early manufacture.

**2.** The manufacture of this lighting fixture was accomplished with modern welding, not hand-forged welds.

# Iron Chandelier, Four Candle 63

From an eighteenth-century design, this wonderfully aged candle holder has been re-created to fill the demands of today's antiques markets and decorators. With four candles providing light, it has just the right accent for an authentic-looking restoration. The construction and the details of age are so good that it's probable that more than one of these lighting fixtures has found a collector's home.

Construction: The vertical shaft is a welded assembly. The top portion is fabricated from square steel bar, twisted and tapered with a rat tail hanging hook forged on its end. The lower end is a 7/16" diameter rod with a shouldered end.

The candle holder web is a welded assembly, fabricated from steel bar. The arms are tapered, arching out from the center to end in an upturned slot. Formed sheet steel candle holders are inserted in the slots and welded in place. All the welds are finish ground and treated to resemble hand forging.

To assemble the shaft to the web, a hole is drilled in the web center. The shaft is inserted through the hole and tack welded in place. A steel washer, slipped over the protruding shaft end on the bottom of the web, is welded in place and finish treated to look like a hand-forged iron assembly.

The illusion of age has been enhanced by purposely leaving irregular edges on the candle holders and a very erratic twisting pattern on the vertical shaft.

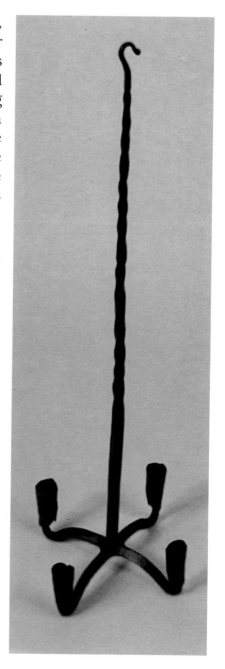

**Height: 20 1/4"**
**Diameter: 7"**

Finish: The lighting device is given a corrosive treatment that rusts and pits the surface. The process virtually eliminates all indications of modern manufacture. To stabilize the corrosion and prevent further rusting, a final staining wax coating is sometimes applied.

## Fake Tip-offs

**1.** On the washer weld located at the center of the web bottom, you will find indentations caused by ball-peen hammering. This has been done to disguise the electric weld and make it appear hand-forged. Ball-peen marks would not be consistent with an original and early manufacture.

**2.** The manufacture of this lighting fixture was accomplished with only modern twentieth-century welding techniques. No hand-forge welding has been used.

*In this view, the fine hanging hook detail is shown with the little curl at its end. Also, notice the irregular pattern in the shaft twist*

*Here the bottom of the web is shown. Notice the weld undercut in the web center. The thickness of the square arm is greater as it moves out from the center weld area.*
*The small diameter outline at the web's center is the welded washer that has been forge treated.*

# Iron Chandelier, Six Candle          **64**

You are looking at one of the nicest wrought-looking chandeliers of eighteenth-century design that I have ever seen. Its ageless elegance is evidenced by the tapered arms, twisted and tapered vertical member and the fine rat tail termination of the hook.

Construction: A 1/2" square steel bar, tapered and twisted to form the graceful center shaft, has its upper end drawn and formed into a rat tail hanging hook. The lower end has a round rod shape with a shouldered end. That end is inserted through the center of the candle arm and a flat steel washer is welded in place. The candle arm assembly has a spider form multiple piece weldment. The spider arms are tapered and arched out to provide a mounting for the candle tubes and their drip pans. The 3 1/2" drip pans are welded to the ends of the arms.The candle tubes have tabs which are inserted through slots in the pans, bent over and welded in place. These welds, like the others, have been finished to resemble hand-forged iron.

Finish: A post-manufacturing corrosive treatment has mildly rusted the metal surface, masking the marks of its modern birth.

**Height: 34 1/4"**
**Diameter: 25"**

## Fake Tip-off

On the original chandelier, forge welding was used extensively to fasten different components together. In this re-creation, electric welding has replaced the time consuming forging process.

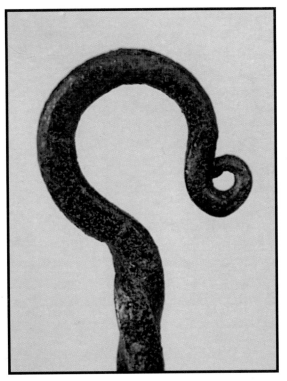

The seemingly hand-forged character of the hanging hook is evident in this illustration. The little curled tail at the end of the hook is great. The illusion of centuries of age is clearly shown with its flaking paint and pitted surface.

The candle holder shown here gives you a good idea of how far the corrosive process can go. The edge of the candle tube is eaten away, as is the edge of the drip pan.

# Iron Chandelier, Ten Candle 65

Ten candle holders in a two-tiered eighteenth-century design make this chandelier a testimony to beauty by candlelight. Its hand-wrought-looking features and aged details have been so faithfully copied that it's almost impossible to tell the difference between the old and the new.

Construction: A 1/2" square steel bar is tapered and twisted to form the upper half of the center shaft. The upper end of this piece is forged into a rat tail hanging hook. The lower end is welded to the web center of the first tier of candle holders. The section of the center shaft located between the two tiers of candles is fabricated from a 5/8" diameter steel rod and the upper end is ground square and welded to the bottom of the upper tier of candles. The lower end has been shouldered, inserted through a hole in the center of the lower tier of candles and a flat steel washer is welded in place. Both tiers of candle holders are constructed in basically the same manner. A spider arm assembly is formed as a multiple piece weldment. The arms are tapered and arched out to provide a mounting for the candle tubes and their drip pans. The 3 1/2" diameter drip pans are welded to the ends of the arms. The candle tubes have tabs which are inserted through slots in the pans, bent over and welded in place. These welds, like the others, have been finished to resemble hand forgings.

**Overall Height: 21"**
**Overall Diameter: 33 1/2"**

Finish: A corrosive treatment is used to create rusting and corrosion pitting. The resulting finish looks centuries old.

## Fake Tip-off

On the original chandelier, forge welding was used to fasten components together. Today electric welding has replaced the time consuming process of hand forging. Look for secondary finishing operations that give the modern process a hand-forged appearance.

*The delicate beauty of the rat tail hook highlights the upper end of the center shaft.*

*The weld joints of the spider are clearly visible in this view of the lower tier candle holder arms.*

# Iron Ball Chandelier

**Overall Height: 21"**                    **Overall Diameter: 33 ¹/₂"**

Although the only known example of this chandelier is said to hang in a European museum, many copies have been made and sold as originals. Its wonderful design and duplication of detail have created an illusion of age that has enabled it to be advertised in leading antiques magazines and newspapers as an antique.

Fooled or not by a dealer's claims of age, buyers have made the ball chandelier a key part of many successful decorating schemes. Whether electrified or lit by candlelight, it remains one of the the most popular chandelier forms.

The weighted center ball with its wrought iron look has three removable candle arm assemblies that hook onto the ball center line.

Construction: The vertical shaft is a steel rod that tapers from a flat hook mount at the top to a thick, bulbous lower end. A large diameter flat washer, a shoulder piece, two ball half-shells, and a bottom dimpled piece are all welded together with the vertical shaft to complete the center assembly. A small flat steel bar hook is forged to the center shaft top for hanging.

A 13/16" wide steel strap is welded and riveted to the center line of the ball. Three arm mounts, welded in place, provide mounts for the candle holder assemblies. All the welds on the ball assembly are flush welds that are ground smooth and treated to resemble hand-forged iron.

The candle holder arms are steel rods with sausage turnings, welded in the center of each arm. Three arms are welded together at one end and a 5/16" strap is wound around the weld joint to provide additional strength. The curled hanger is, again, a welded assembly. On the outer end of the arms are welded 3 7/8" iron sheet drip pans and candle tubes.

Finish: The entire chandelier is given a corrosive treatment that produces rust and pitting, simulating centuries of age. A final waxy coating is sometimes applied to stabilize the corrosion.

## Fake Tip-offs

**1.** Because this chandelier has been made for so many years, there are many variations of detail and quality of finish. You will find them rusted beyond belief. Big scales of rust, holes corroded through and edges eaten away are common. On others, the attention to detail is amazing. You will find no evidence of welding because a simulated hand-forged finish has eliminated it.

**2.** On the museum original, the arm turnings are a hand-forged part of the arm. On this re-creation they are separate pieces, welded in place. Minute machined grooves are evident in the turned surface, indicating modern manufacture. Remember, welding of this type is a twentieth-century manufacturing technique.

**3.** In this close-up view of the ball bottom, you see an indented groove where the bottom shell meets the dimpled piece. This is created by the welding and the clean-up grinding process.

*Here you can see the undercut of the welding operation and the indentation of the clean-up grinding on the sconce arm.*

# Tin Chandelier, Six Candle 67

An American design, this six-arm chandelier exhibits a typically high degree of colonial design and workmanship. Its sheet metal and soldered construction has made a very sturdy and interesting lighting device. To increase its stability while hanging, the bottom cone is given additional weight.

Construction: Two similar cones of formed sheet steel are soldered together to make the main body of the chandelier. The cones are filled with sand and pebbles for weight. The finial and the steel vertical column are soldered to the top of the center column. The six candle arms are solder fastened, equally spaced around the lower body cone. The candle drip pans are riveted to the arms and the solder holds the candle tubes in place.

Finish: A cracked red primer coat and a top coat of grey-green serves as the final finish. Its cracked and grungy looking paint gives the appearance of great age.

**Overall Height: 24 1/4"**
**Overall Diameter: 20 1/4"**

**Fake Tip-off**

Red primer would not have been used on an authentic antique.

# Dutch Crown, Four Candle 68

Called Dutch crowns by d'Allemangne, these wrought-iron devices originally were part of a sixteenth- or seventeenth-century food pantry. They were hung from the ceiling of a room. Meat and game hung from the hooks while candles supplied the light.

You will find these today as a focal point in food preparation areas, used for hanging dried flowers, herbs or even pots and pans.

Construction: A 1 3/4" wide steel band forms the main structural member of this crown. Riveted to this is a twisted steel rod framework that arches up to the center, where it is welded to a hanging eye. The weld area is ground smooth and blended into the center eye. In the middle of each arched rod is a flattened and twisted section. At the lower end of the framework each rod end is tapered and formed into a hook. Above each rivet four small curls of steel are welded and finished to look hand forged. Candle holders with 3 1/2" diameter drip pans are welded to similar decorative hooks located in the center of each framework quadrant. The holders will take up to a 7/8" diameter candle.

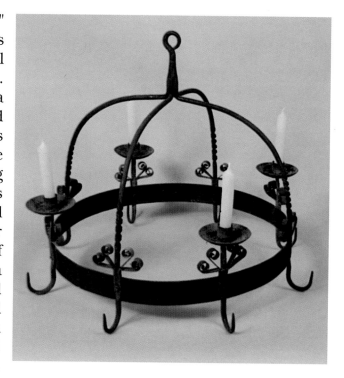

**Overall Height: 22 3/4"**
**Overall Diameter: 18 3/4"**

Finish: The entire fixture has been given a rusted and corroded, pitted look that imparts a centuries-old appearance.

## Fake Tip-off

Look for added weld material at the junction of the decorative curls. For additional information see the spikes, racks and crowns, data sheet #109, Fake Tip-offs, #1.

# Floor Standard, Rush/Candle Light   69

Rush light and candle combinations are relatively rare. You almost never find a floor standard with a mounted adjustable combination. In areas of the world where candle light is still used, fakers have forged this original-looking floor-standing lighting device.

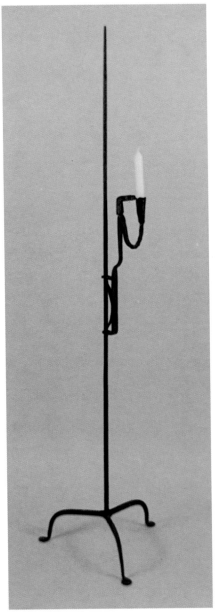

**Overall Height: 53"**
**Light Assembly Width: 4"**

Construction: The floor standard has a 7/16" diameter round steel rod center shaft that supports the light assembly. The upper end is tapered and rounded off. The bottom end is shouldered and inserted through a hole in the base. The base and shaft are then assembled together by welding that gives a hand-forged look. The steel rod base is again welded and finished with a hand-forged look. Its arched, tapered legs terminate in 1" diameter penny shaped feet.

The adjustable rush light and candle holder assembly is fabricated from steel sheet and bar. The candle holder is welded to a twisted curved bar that has one of the rush holder jaws welded on the other end. The other jaw is part of the frame and spring assembly. The top slide of the frame is sheet steel rivet forged to the frame and bottom slide. An elliptical spring riveted to the frame provides two pressure points that hold the assembly in place.

Finish: The entire lighting fixture is given a corrosive treatment designed to create an aged surface finish. The rusting and pitting resulting from this process are sometimes stabilized by a staining wax final coating.

## Fake Tip-offs

**1.** Electric welding has been used to create complex structural shapes that would have been hand-forged in the original. These can be determined by comparing the characteristics of hand-forged joints to welded joints.

**2.** Examine the wear surface. You will find, for the most part, that they are free of any appreciable wear. This is highly unlikely for an eighteenth-century original.

**3.** A point to remember: many floor standards are interchangeable, making many different combinations possible.

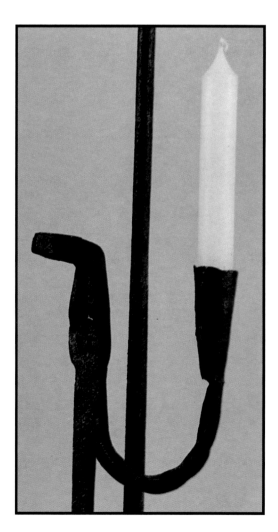

*The corrosion in this view of the rush holder and candle counterweight suggests centuries of use.*

# Floor Standard, Candle Type 1 $\quad$ 70

With one of the earliest designs, this standard has a heavy construction that makes it very stable and unlikely to tip over during the adjustment of its candles. A unique four-spring design provides the pressure necessary to hold the candle adjustment.

Construction: A 1/2" round steel rod forms the center shaft of this floor standard. The shaft, topped with a round finial, has its bottom turned to a shoulder that has been inserted through a hole in the base and welded in place. The weld is then hammered to give it a hand-forged look.

The base is fabricated from sheet steel and welded in a three-legged configuration. The three legs arch from the center and end in slightly flared feet.

The candle holder is fabricated from sheet steel. The rectangular frame material size is 1/8" thick x 1" wide. The four springs have their ends bent at 90 degrees and riveted to the frame. The two candle tubes are riveted in place.

Finish: The entire lighting device is treated with a corrosive process that dramatically ages it. A final surface coat of staining wax is occasionally used to stabilize the corrosion.

**Fake Tip-off**

For the fake tip-offs that apply to this floor standard, see data sheet #69.

**Overall Height: 46 $^5/_8$"**
**Candle Holder Width: 10 $^3/_8$"**

# Floor Standard, Candle Type 2     71

This wrought-iron-looking floor standard holds an adjustable dual candle holder, moved by exerting an upward pressure on the two elliptical springs inside the rectangular frame. Lower travel of the candle holder is limited by the taper on the standard's upper half diameter. The turnings on the standard serve as transitions for material shapes and sizes. The lower square bar portion of the vertical shaft serves to unite the legs with the tapered upper rod.

Probably an eighteenth-century device, the classical style of its design is timeless. You now have a "Fabulous Fake" re-creation that rivals the original for craftsmanship and appearance, perfect for contemporary restorations.

Construction: The standard's upper vertical steel rod has a maximum diameter of 3/8". The lower section is fabricated from a 1/2" square steel bar which, with a shouldered lower end, is inserted through a center hole in the turning and sheet steel base. It is welded in place and then hammered to give a hand-forged appearance. The gracefully formed sheet steel legs terminate in 1 1/4" diameter penny feet.

The adjustable candle holder has a patterned and decorated cross arm that supports two riveted candle holders. A rectangular frame is rivet-forged to the arm along with the elliptical springs and two accessory hooks.

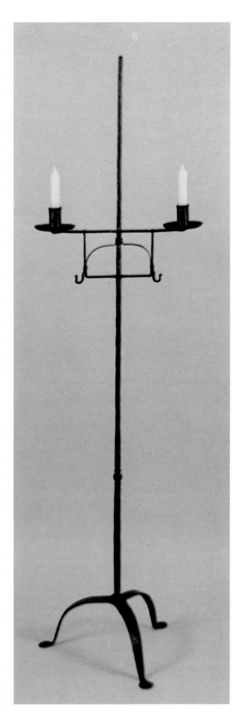

**Overall Height: 54"**
**Base Height: 5 1/4"**
**Overall Width: 15 5/8"**

Finish: The entire adjustable candle holder and floor standard is given a corrosive treatment to create a surface finish that duplicates centuries of age and wear. A final waxy coating is applied to stabilize the surface and prevent further rusting.

**Fake Tip-offs**

**1.** The floor standard shaft construction looks like it was hand forged from one piece of iron bar. However, in all probability, it is a multi-piece welded assembly. Look for indications of added weld material and electric grinding. *Because the candle holder assembly is removable, other standard-holder combinations are entirely possible.*

**2.** On an original antique, considerable wear should be evident on the spring contact surfaces and on the bottoms of the three penny feet.

*This close-up of the candle holder highlights the beautifully simple design and close attention paid to detail.*

# Floor Standard, Candle Type 3    **72**

This adjustable candle holder has a double elliptical spring to grip the center rod of the standard. To move the holder, an outward pressure is exerted on the two springs, allowing it to move to a new position. This has to be one of the more stable designs, with four points of spring pressure. The floor standard is the same one as shown on data sheet #71. It is a steel construction with a very graceful design. Nostalgic candlelight, historically accurate with a centuries-old look... but manufactured today.

Construction: The standard's upper vertical steel rod has a maximum diameter of 3/8". This rod allows for the candle holder to travel approximately 25". The section below the decorative turnings is fabricated from 1/2" steel bar, which, with a shouldered lower end, is inserted through a center hole in the lower turning and sheet steel base. It is welded and then hammered to look like hand forging. The gracefully formed sheet steel legs terminate in 1 1/4" diameter penny feet.

The candle holder frame is made of steel bar. Two double ended elliptical springs are riveted to the lower half of the frame. Two 4 5/8" diameter drip pans, with 1 1/16" diameter riveted candle tubes, complete the frame assembly.

**Overall Height: 51 1/4"**
**Base Height: 5 1/4"**
**Overall Width: 14 1/4"**

Finish: The illusion of age is the crowning achievement of the fakers who created this lighting device. Tooling and other marks of manufacture have disappeared under the corrosion and pitting of a special chemical process. A final coating of staining wax is used to stabilize rust and give the surface that wonderful satiny feeling of old iron.

## Fake Tip-off

Wear surfaces should be examined closely. An authentically old device would show the soft fuzzy grey surface texture of high wear on the bottoms of the penny feet. The spring contact surfaces should also have some indication of wear.

*Surface corrosion and pitting is obvious in this close-up view of the candle holder. The hand forged look can be seen where the rectangular frame tapers towards the drip pan and candle tube.*

# Floor Standard, Candle Type 4     73

A three-section metal curl, gracefully curved legs terminating in penny feet and a dramatically heavy center turning are the dominant features of this standard. The weight of these and the rest of the assembly makes this a very stable lighting device. The dual candle holder is held firmly in place by its two elliptical retaining springs. The candle holder bottoms against a shoulder near the top of the vertical shaft and is free to rotate 360 degrees.

Construction: The tapered round steel rod of the vertical standard is welded to a square section of steel bar and finished by hand grinding to blend the two shapes. The decorative turnings of the vertical shaft are welded in place and finished by hand grinding. All the welds, including the steel curls and steel rod base, have received surface treatments to simulate a hand-forged condition. The adjustable frame has a pattern-decorated cross arm supporting two candle holders riveted in place. A "U" shaped frame is rivet-forged to the arm, along with the two elliptical pressure springs. The drip pans of the candle holders have scalloped edges, each with ten 18" diameter holes. The rolled steel candle holders will accept up to a 1" diameter candle.

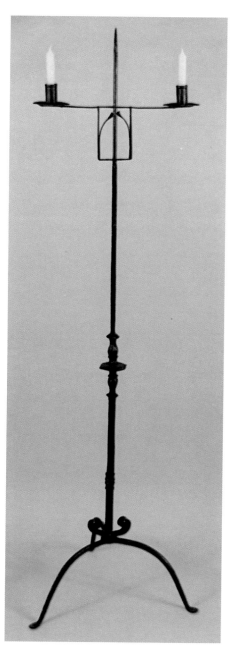

**Overall Height: 60"**
**Holder Height: 52 ³/₄"**
**Overall Width: 17"**

Finish: The entire candle holder and floor standard is given a corrosive treatment to create an aged surface finish of rust and pitting. A final staining wax finish is sometimes applied to stabilize the surface and prevent further rusting.

## Fake Tip-offs

**1.** The heavy cast turning on the vertical shaft does not mate squarely with the square bar section.

**2.** Close examination of the construction will expose electrically welded areas which are, of course, a twentieth-century development.

**3.** The bottoms of the feet and the spring contact surface do not show any wear. A real antique would have a considerable amount.

*Highlighted in this view is the simple design, functional and yet elegant at the same time.*

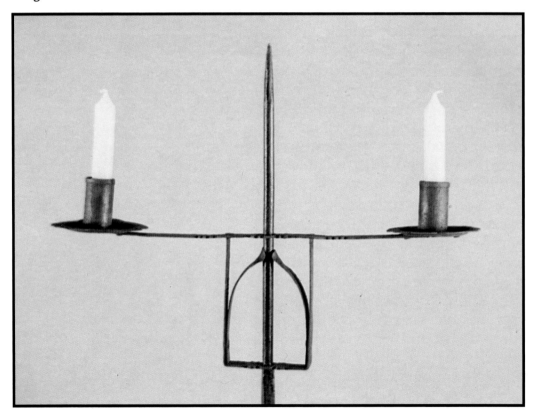

# Iron Candelabra, Two Candle  74

Good design makes this candelabra a worth-while addition to any decorating scheme, equally at home in a modern or historical setting. It has been re-created in a fake edition of its original form. The three-legged metal stand provides a fair amount of travel for the adjustable dual candle holder. The turning on the center shaft is the lower limit of the candle holder's travel. The two elliptical leaf springs, located inside the "U" shaped frame of the candle supply the pressure needed to hold the candle adjustment.

Construction: Steel sheet and rod are the major materials in this assembly. The base is cut from steel sheet and formed with gentle curves into the penny footed stand. A preformed shoulder on the lower end of the

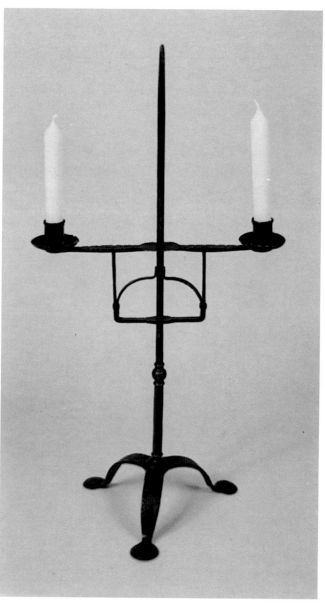

**Overall Height: 22 1/2"**
**Overall Width: 11 1/2"**
**Base Diameter: 10"**

center shaft is inserted through a hole in the base and welded in place. The turnings on the shaft are precast and welded to the shaft at assembly. The candle holder arm is fabricated from sheet steel notched in a decorative pattern. The "U" shaped frame is rivet-forged to the arm, along with the elliptical springs and the two accessory hooks. A candle holder with a 2" drip pan is riveted at the end of each arm. The center shaft's probable construction sequence is as follows: a 3/8" square bar is welded to a section of round rod and finished by hand grinding. The cast turning that limits candle holder travel is then assembled on the rod, bottoming against the 3/8" square, and welded in place.

Finish: The entire candle holder is given a corrosive treatment after a deburring operation. The resulting rusted finish looks centuries old. A staining wax final coating is applied to stabilize the finish and prevent further rusting.

**Fake Tip-offs**

**1.** Close examination of its construction details will expose electrically welded joints. This type of welding is a twentieth-century production method.

**2.** The penny feet and the spring contact area do not exhibit the wear that would be expected on an actual antique. If you find no wear, it is obviously a fake.

*This enlarged view shows a corner of the rectangular frame, the elliptical spring and a hand-forged accessory hook.*

# Swivel Arm Candle Holder

## 75

Originally constructed of heavy iron bar and sheet, this candle holder was designed to swivel between two wall mounted eyes or similar brackets. With its long reach, the light source moved out into the living area when needed, increasing its effectiveness. When not required, it could be folded back, out of the way. The original design of this fake looks early and rugged enough to have been used in some of the world's great castles and other stone buildings.

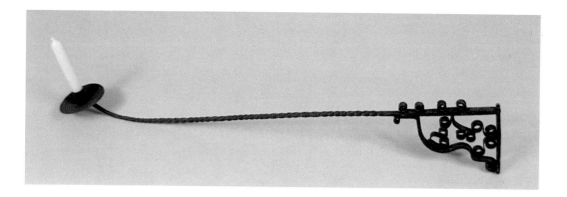

**Overall Length: 34 ³/₈"**

Construction: A long twisted and tapered steel bar forms the arm of this assembly. A 3/4" diameter candle holder and 3 7/8" diameter drip pan are riveted on the small tapered end of the arm. The other end of the arm is inserted through a hole in the pivot bar and hammer forged to make a permanent assembly. An irregularly formed diagonal brace is riveted and forged to the assembly.

The scroll work on the bracket end of the candle holder is made of sheet steel. Each loop is formed separately and welded to others to create the scroll configurations shown in the illustrations. The welded end is ground into a shouldered shank that is inserted through holes in the frame of the candle holder and forged or welded in place.

Finish: The entire candle holder is given a corrosive treatment after a deburring operation. The resulting rusted finish looks centuries old. A staining wax final coating is sometimes applied to stabilize the surface and prevent further rusting.

**Fake Tip-off**

The assembly and electric welding of the scroll assemblies is clearly shown in this illustration. The scroll on the right hand side of the bracket is plug-welded in position. The top scroll is fastened in position using the shouldered shank of the inside scroll as a rivet and an electrically welded flat washer as the forged tail.

*The bottom of the candle holder in this view clearly shows the riveting assembly method and the high degree of realism obtained with the finish.*

# Iron Candle Holder

The fake iron construction and stiletto profile of this candle holder make a very dramatic statement. It would look equally appropriate in a modern or colonial setting. The fact that it looks hand-forged adds additional character to the piece.

Construction: A rolled steel candle socket is welded to the tapered end of the 3/8" square stem. A finish grinding operation blends the socket into the stem to simulate a total forging fabrication. The bottom of the stem is formed into a shoulder. The small shoulder diameter is then assembled to the base pan and leg assembly and welded in place. A sheet steel leg assembly is formed to a 5 1/2" overall diameter, then riveted to the pan.

Finish: The entire candle holder is given a corrosive treatment to create artificial age. A final staining wax coating is applied to stabilize the surface and prevent further rusting.

**Fake Tip-offs**

**1.** Electric welding has been used in place of the time consuming hand-forged welds. Look for indications of added weld material and hand grinding. They are sure signs of modern manufacture.

**2.** There should be ample evidence of wear on the bottom of the feet. Lack of wear is a cause for concern about its age.

**Overall Height: 14 3/8"**
**Drip Pan Diameter: 4 1/8"**

# Alpine Torch Holder

**Overall Height: 18 $^7/_8$"**
**Base Pan Depth: 6 $^1/_8$"**
**Base Pan Width: 5 $^3/_{16}$"**

Called a torch holder by Henry Rene d'Allemagne and a candle holder by others, this is a great re-creation of a seventeenth-century Alpine lighting device. The hand-forged-looking details, meticulously accurate, and a corroded finish make it hard to distinguish the real from the reproduced. A very decorative piece that probably has found its way into more than one collection.

Construction: Eleven pieces of steel sheet and rod make up this assembly. The round vertical member has a shoulder formed on its lower end. It is here that the base plate, the rat tail spring support and the footed legs are assembled. The shoulder end is then hammered over, fastening the four sections together. The vertical member has two flattened areas that are used to mount the spring and the torch or candle ring. Along with rat tail handles and decorative pieces, they are riveted in place. The rat tails are all hand-forged, with very decorative curls and swirls. The handmade character of this lighting device is important. Nowhere do you find evidence of machine-made parts or fabrication. Tooling marks and electric welding burns have all been eliminated by the corrosive finishing process.

Finish: The lighting device is deburred to remove all sharp edges. A corrosive process is then used to recreate the 300-year-old finish that you see in the close-up pictures. Its rusting and pitted finish have completely eliminated the marks of modern manufacturing. These pictures show a fairly dry, rusty finish. However, more recently manufactured pieces have a staining wax final coating that prevents further rusting and adds a little grime to the metal surface.

### Fake Tip-off

A true antique lighting device would have a flat spot worn on the bottom of its curled front foot. This torch holder has the material form as it was first made, with no sign of wear.

# Iron Rush Light/Candle Holder     78

This lighting device provides a combination of two light sources. The first is rushes. The plier-like jaws are used to hold grease soaked rushes, with the socket arm providing the necessary counterweight for firm holding. The second source is candles, used in the counterweight socket.

The re-creation of this early lighting device, while historically correct, does not lend itself to modern living very well. You might burn your house down from the rush sparks, and the candle drippings certainly make a mess.

Construction: It is difficult to determine how many pieces of steel make up this device. The hand-forged look has been carried to its highest form, covering the marks of modern manufacture. However, let's start our review at the top with the rush holder jaws. They are made of flattened steel, interlocking with a center hinge pin. The fixed jaw drops into a round rod shape with a shouldered end, which in turn is riveted to the base spider. The movable jaw has a round rod arm attached, with a candle socket at the end. The socket is a hand formed piece of sheet steel, rolled into a cone shape and welded into a slot cut in the arm end. A dimension worth noting is from the center line of the pin to the end of the jaws, 2 3/8". The opening of the candle socket measures 13/16" in diameter.

The base spider has a flat center section with the edges hammered over to form a recess for the vertical shaft fastening and the

**Overall Height: 10"**
**Base Diameter: 7 1/2"**

legs that gently taper out, curving to meet the flat penny feet. The seams on the underside of the legs have been welded closed and finished by hand grinding. The feet seem to be pre-cut and welded to the ends of the tapered legs.

Finish: Deburring, corrosive processing and a final staining wax coating complete the manufacturing of this device. The unique method of creating a hand-forged look with a finishing process really works well. The close-up view of the spider base illustrates this.

**Fake Tip-off**

The bottom of the three penny shaped feet have no sign of wear. A truly old device would exhibit serious wear.

# Iron Rush Light/Candle Holder　79

A similar combination of rush light and candle holder is shown on data sheet #78. The primary difference between the two is that this one has a drip tray under the candle tube, making it more useful in a modern living environment. The interlocking jaws originally held burning grease-soaked rushes. However, we do not recommend using that as a source of light because of the fire hazard. Use up your candle stubs and enjoy the eighteenth-century design.

Construction; Made of modern steel and manufactured using modern methods, it simulates an eighteenth-century hand-forging. The rush holder jaws are made of flattened steel, interlocked with a center hinge pin. The fixed jaw drops into a twisted square bar shape with a shouldered end that in turn is riveted to the spider base. The movable jaw has a twisted square bar attached with a candle socket at the end. The socket is made of rolled sheet steel and riveted to the arm. The candle drip tray is 2 3/8" in diameter and the socket will take a 13/16" diameter candle.

The base spider has a flat center section that has its edges hammered over to form a recess for the vertical shaft fastening.

**Overall Height: 10 ³/₈"**
**Overall Base Diameter: 8"**

In the close-up below, notice the material seams that run towards the feet have most of their length welded closed. The legs gently taper out, curving to meet the flat penny feet, which also appear to be welded in place.

Finish: Deburring, corrosive processing and a final staining wax coating complete the manufacturing of this lighting device. The idea of creating a hand-forged look with a finishing process works well.

### Fake Tip-off

The bottoms of the penny shaped feet are not flat. They have material seams and lumps. They do not have any of the wear you would expect to find on a real antique.

# Adjustable Iron Candlestick          80

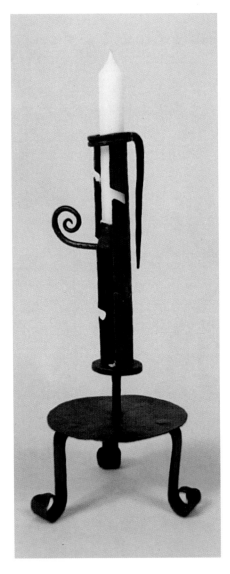

**Overall Height: 12"**
**Overall Base Diameter: 6"**

The seventeenth century lives on in this early design. I find it amazing that modern electric welding techniques can so closely duplicate hand forging. In places where hammer or forge welding was used on the original, electric welding and a finish grinding operation have been substituted. The final corrosive process removes all the final finish grinding marks and it truly looks hand forged. Its hand-forged and rusted look is appropriate for a candlestick that is supposed to be 300 years old.

Construction: The assembly of this adjustable candle holder is accomplished by riveting and electric welding eleven pieces of steel sheet and rod together. The 4 3/4" diameter drip pan stands 2 7/8" high on preformed riveted legs. The sharp pointed handle at the top of the candle tube will fit over a chair back or in a bracket hole, both designed to hold the candlestick upright safely. The forged curled handle on the left side of the tube is attached to a movable plug in the tube center. Predetermined candle settings are obtained, by positioning the handle in the tube's angled slots. The inside tube diameter will accommodate up to a 1" diameter candle.

Finish: The candle holder, after being deburred to remove all the sharp edges, undergoes a corrosive process to recreate the 300-year-old look that you see in the illustration. Its rusting, pitted finish has completely eliminated the marks of modern manufacturing.

**Fake Tip-offs**

**1.** The effects of modern welding can be seen inside the candle tube at both ends. Look for burn-out areas where the steel has melted from the high heat of welding. Also, the welding process deposits additional material, which is another indication of its modern construction.

**2.** The bottoms of the three curled feet show only a trace of wear. If this device were truly old, these surfaces would show years of wear.

# Adjustable Iron Candle Holder 81

The delicate and graceful lines of this candle holder indicate its probable design origin as early nineteenth-century European. The spring-loaded candle holder and the top candle guide, as well as the base standard, have been re-created with an appropriate aged, rusted finish. It's tough to tell...

Construction: This assembly consists of ten pieces of steel sheet and rod. The base is assembled using the 1/4" square vertical rod as a rivet. A shoulder is turned on the lower rod end. The cupped stiffener plate, along with the 6 3/8" diameter base plate and the leg spider, are assembled in sequence on the shoulder end of the shaft. The shaft end is then transformed into a rivet head by using a flat washer electrically welded to its end. The right hand curved member under the candle is the spring that provides the pressure to hold the candle in position. The candle tube will accommodate up to a 3/4" diameter candle.

Finish: After the irregular hand trimmed edges are deburred, the candle holder is given a corrosive process that gives it that original aged look. Further rusting is prevented by a final staining wax coating.

**Overall Height: 17 1/2"**
**Overall Base Diameter: 8"**

**Fake Tip-offs**

**1.** You should be able to notice in the close-up illustration what look like hand forging marks close to the center. Actually it indicates that the spider is a welded assembly, which makes a lot of sense since it would save a lot of material.

**2.** What looks like the end of the shaft, hand forged to a riveted assembly, is actually an electrically welded washer. This is twentieth century all the way.

# Diamond Base Alpine Holder          82

A replication of an eighteenth-century Alpine design, this device provides a sturdy platform for a modern accent of candlelight. A candle is held in place by a long flat spring with a small loop handle. The bent-over top of the vertical twisted column serves as a carrying handle and, in earlier times, provided a convenient method for hanging it on the back of a chair.

Construction: Nine pieces of sheet steel make up this candle holder. Let's start our review at the candle ring. It is a formed loop welded to a forged arm, which in turn is riveted to the twisted upright. With the spring in place, it will hold a 1" diameter candle. The spring drops down to the base, where it is bent 90 degrees and welded to the twisted upright. The upright goes through a hole in the base plate and leg spider and is welded over a flat washer to serve as the primary fastener for the leg spider. The spider is a welded assembly, using two strips of sheet steel with the feet as bent tabs hammered flat and thin. The base plate has a slightly rolled up lip that helps retain any melted wax.

Finish: Deburring, corrosive aging and a wax top coat combine to make another fabulous re-creation believable.

**Overall Height: 9 1/4"**
**Overall Width: 5 1/4"**
**Overall Length: 5 1/2"**

**Fake Tip-offs**

**1.** A flat washer and electric welding have been used to terminate the bottom of the upright. An antique would have been hand forged.

**2.** As on many of the other devices, the accumulated years of wear have not happened to this fake Alpine holder. The feet show little use.

**3.** The corrosion patterns are not the same for all parts of the holder. The rusting should be evenly distributed and it is not. Some of the metal parts were made from pre-rusted steel.

# Heart Base Alpine Holder

# 83

This candle holder is similar to the one pictured on data sheet #82. The heart shaped base plate of this holder is the only difference. It is an eighteenth-century design manufactured in 1992. Looking at it, you would shake your head and swear it was at least 200 years old... it's that good. The irregular hand-cut edges and lack of anything straight and true seem to confirm that illusion.

**Overall Height: 8 3/4"**
**Overall Width: 5 1/4"**
**Overall Length: 5 1/2"**

Construction: Nine pieces of hand forged sheet steel make up this candle holder. Let's start the review at the candle ring. It is a formed loop with the seam side welded to a forged arm, which in turn is riveted to the twisted upright. With the spring in place, it will hold a 1" diameter candle. The flat sheet metal spring, with its forged rat tail handle, drops down to the base where it is bent 90 degrees and welded to the twisted upright. The upright, inserted through a hole in the base plate and the leg spider, is plug welded, to serve as the primary fastener for the leg spider. The spider is made from two strips of sheet, welded together. The legs and feet are hand formed, hammered flat and tapered to the outer edge of the feet. The base plate has a slightly rolled up edge that forms a drip pan for melted wax. Here again, all the welded joints have been made to look hand forged.

Finish: Deburring, corrosive treating and a wax top coat combine to make the illusion of age believable.

**Fake Tip-offs**

**1.** The bottom view clearly shows the plug weld used on the lower end of the upright. The electric welding used here is a technical development of this century.

**2.** The spring and the upright member are clearly electrically welded at the base plate. These would have been hand-forged welds on a real antique.

# Spiral Candlestick

## 84

The eighteenth-century look of this spiral candle holder is quite appealing. It is even a practical light source today, with the spiral candle tube providing a variable light height.

Construction: Ten pieces of riveted and welded steel make up this assembly. The drip pan stands 2 3/4" high on three legs. The legs have 7/8" diameter penny feet and edges that have been bent over and hammered flat. There are twenty-one indentations around the pan edge which, other than providing some rigidity, are purely decorative. The round tab on the left side of the candle tube is fastened to a plug in the center of the spiral. This provides for the adjustment of candle height when rotated. The tin curled rod at the top of the tube serves as a handle and a means of hanging the candle holder on a chair. The spiral inside diameter will accommodate up to a 1" diameter candle. The tube handle is electric-welded to the spiral and finish ground. In spite of that process, it has a hand-forged look.

**Overall Height: 11 1/2"**
**Base Diameter: 4 1/4"**

Finish: After a deburring operation that removes all the sharp edges, a corrosive process is used to create a rusted surface. Look at that finish... fantastic age. There is even a rusted-though hole at the edge of the pan.

## Fake Tip-offs

**1.** The weld joint of the handle to the spiral tube shows a typical electric weld undercut. This is a condition where the material diameter of the handle sharply but smoothly necks down to meet the end of the spiral tube. This condition would not be found on a truly hand-forged antique.

**2.** A flat washer with electric welding has been used to assemble the base to the spiral tube. The welded washer has been treated to resemble part of an old riveted joint.

# Wood Base Rush Holder 85

The hand-forged look of the iron jaws and the offset counterweight of this rush holder lend testimony to a much simpler time.

Construction: This device is made from a 1/4" square steel bar. The 1/4" wide jaws are interlocking, with a rivet hinge pin. They measure 2 1/16" from the hinge pin to the jaw end. A roughly formed counterweight ball, 9/16" in diameter, is created at the end of the offset arm. The square steel shank of the holder is hammered into a turned wood base. The dimensions and material sizes will vary from piece to piece, but the manufacturing process is constant.

**Overall Height: 9 ³/4"**
**Base Diameter: 3 ¹/2"**

Finish: After a deburring process, the entire steel portion of the rush holder is given a corrosive treatment. The entire lighting device is given a final staining wax coating to stabilize the surface and to add a little color to the wood base. Thus a great illusion of age is created.

### Fake Tip-offs

**1.** The rush holding jaws are very tight. They have little wear on the hinge point and many are rusted shut because of the corrosive aging process. Jaws on truly old rush holders will show their age in a loose joint and worn surface.

**2.** The new wood base is easiest to recognize as fake. It may have cracks from the core to the base. The bottom surface has not been disguised very well. There is no worn look of old wood.

# Wood Base Spiral Candlestick 86

A strip of crudely twisted steel and a plug traveling around the spiral twist provide continuous adjustment for this candlestick. The upper end of the twist serves as a handle suitable for carrying or hanging on the back of a chair. The lower end of the twist is hammered into a turned block of wood, providing a very stable base for this device. This design dates to the mid-eighteenth century.

Construction: A strip of soft steel, 5/8" wide, forms the twisted body of this candlestick. The 13/16" inside diameter allows a smaller diameter steel plug with a finger knob to travel up and down the spiral. The upper end of the twist is cut square to the body. The lower end of the twist is forged to a sharp point formed parallel to the longitudinal axis of the twisted tube. It is then hammered into a crude 2 3/8" high wooden base. Tropical fruitwoods and mahogany serve as base materials. Dimensions and material sizes will vary from piece to piece. Design changes can and will occur. The wooden base size and turnings are never constant. There are also many different plug and knob or tab combinations. The handle at the top of the twist is subject to the design whim of the faker.

**Overall Height: 9 $^1/_2$"**
**Base Diameter: 4 $^1/_{16}$"**

Finish: After a deburring process, the steel portion of this candlestick is given a corrosive treatment. The wooden base is also treated with stains and burns to simulate years of use. The entire candlestick is given a final staining wax coating to stabilize the surface. The illusion continues.

## Fake Tip-off

The new wood base is the easiest part to recognize as fake. It may have new wood cracks from the core to the outside edge of the base. Also, its bottom surface has not been disguised very well. There is none of the soft, worn look of old wood. The surface is new, with its only marking being sanding and the tool marks of the modern manufacturer.

*A finger tab is used here instead of a knob. Also note the burning on the wooden base, designed to create grain checking and the appearance of great age.*

# Plain Iron Hog Scrapers 87

Hog scraper candlesticks abound in many shapes, forms and sizes. Almost any book showing colonial room settings will probably have one or more hog scrapers in it. Back on the early farms, the base of this candlestick form was used to scrape the bristles off hogs at butchering time. Now with that aspect of everyday life gone, it is back to the table as a candlestick only.

Construction: Sheet steel, .074" thick, is formed into an inverted saucer shaped base to which the candle tube assembly is attached. The candle tube is formed of rolled sheet steel, held in place by the brazed top cupped flange and the lower support flange. The push-up assembly is inserted in the lower end of the candle tube and a flanged stud is electrically welded in place to cap the tube end. The candle tube is then assembled to the base and fastened with a thin jam nut.

| | Size A | Size B | Size C |
|---|---|---|---|
| **Overall Height:** | 8 1/8" | 10 5/8" | 11 3/4" |
| **Base Diameter:** | 4 3/4" | 4 3/4" | 5" |

Finish: After a deburring operation that removes all the sharp edges, the excess solder and braze material are removed. The entire candlestick is then given a corrosive treatment, rusting its entire surface. A final staining wax coating is applied to stabilize the finish and prevent further rusting.

**Fake Tip-offs**

**1.** Electric welding has been used for the flange stud assembly. See data sheet #90 for a close-up picture of the method. Antique hog scrapers did not use welding. The stud has modern machine-cut threads, not the coarse hand-cut type of original antiques.

**2.** The top of the candle tube on the fake has been rolled over to captivate the top cupped flange. Most antique hog scrapers have no rolled over flanges.

**3.** These candlesticks are made of steel. On authentic antiques, tin and iron sheet would have been used. The steel used on the base is many times thicker than that used on real antiques.

*This close-up view of the candlestick bottom surface shows the degree of corrosion and surface pitting.*

# Faceted Band Hog Scraper, Small      **88**

On the farm, at butchering time, it was used to scrape off hog bristles. However, today this simple tin candlestick serves only as a light source. The one pictured here is one of the smallest you will ever see. Its brass wedding band ring and collar feature a faceted design that is quite unusual for a hog scraper.

Construction: Sheet steel .045" thick is formed into an inverted saucer-shaped base, to which the candle tube assembly is attached. The candle tube is rolled sheet steel, held in place by the top cupped flange, the brass wedding band and the lower faceted brass ring. The brass pieces are soldered in place with the top edge of the candle tube rolled over in the cup flange and brazed. A push-up assembly is inserted into the candle tube center and held in place with a finger tab. In the lower end of the candle tube, a flanged stud is inserted and electrically welded in place. The entire assembly is put together and secured with a thin jam nut.

Finish: The assembly is deburred to remove the sharp edges. The excess solder is removed and then the entire candlestick is given a corrosive processing to create a rusty, centuries-old look. The final finish is a wax coating that stabilizes the finish and prevents further rusting.

### Fake Tip-off

See data sheet #87 for a complete description

**Overall Height:  6" approx.**
**Base Diameter:  4" approx.**

# Wedding Band Hog Scrapers 89

This is the first wedding band hog scraper candlestick the fakers made. Its smooth golden brass ring, looking very much like a wedding band, gives this its distinctive name. The hog scraper is rugged, practical and yet a decorative colonial-looking accessory. There are three sizes in this style. Their major dimensional differences are listed in the following chart.

|  | Size A | Size B | Size C |
|---|---|---|---|
| **Overall Height:** | 9 $1/8$" | 10 $5/8$" | 11 $5/8$" |
| **Base Diameter:** | 4 $5/8$" | 4 $3/4$" | 5" |

Construction: Sheet steel, .064" thick, is formed into an inverted saucer-shaped base, to which the candle tube assembly is attached. The candle tube is formed of rolled sheet steel, held in place by the top cupped flange with hanging tab, the central, shouldered plain brass ring and the lower steel support flange.

The individual pieces of this candlestick are assembled and bonded together using a variety of methods. The first is solder, which is used to hold the brass ring in position. The second is brazing, used to hold the top and bottom flanges in place. The third is electric welding. After the push-up assembly is inserted in the lower end of the candle tube, a flanged stud, welded in place, caps off the end. The candle tube is then assembled to the base and fastened with a thin jam nut.

Finish: After a deburring operation that removes all the sharp edges, the excess solder and braze material are removed. The entire candlestick is then given a corrosive treatment that creates a rusted surface. A final wax coating is applied to stabilize the finish.

### Fake Tip-off

See data sheet #87 for a complete description.

*The brazing shown here is used to assemble the flanges to the tubes. The rolled edge of the candle tube can be seen clearly.*

# Faceted Band Hog Scrapers 90

Here is another style of faceted wedding band hog scraper candlestick. The distinguishing feature of these is that brass is used only in the wedding band around the center of the candle tube. Used singularly, in pairs or in a grouping of different sizes, they create a subtle light source that is historically correct.

There are three sizes in this style and the major dimensional differences are shown in the following chart.

|  | Size A | Size B | Size C |
|---|---|---|---|
| Overall Height: | 8 $3/8$" | 10 $3/8$" | 12 $5/8$" |
| Base Diameter: | 4 $3/8$" | 4 $3/4$" | 5 $1/4$" |

Construction: Sheet steel, .045" thick, is formed into an inverted saucer-shaped base, to which the candle tube assembly is attached. The candle tube is formed of rolled sheet steel, held in place by the top cupped flange with hanging tab, the central brass (wedding band) ring and the lower steel support flange.

A variety of bonding methods are used in the assembly of this candlestick. Solder is used to fasten the brass ring in place, while brazing is used on most of the candle tube pieces. A push-up assembly is inserted into the candle tube center and held in place with a finger tab. In the lower end of the candle tube, a flanged stud is inserted and electrically welded in place. The entire assembly is put together and secured with a thin jam nut.

Finish: All the sharp edges are removed by a deburring operation. The excess solder and braze material are removed. The candlestick is then given a corrosive process that creates that marvelous rust. After the right amount of corrosion, a final wax coating is applied to stabilize the finish, preventing any further rusting.

## Fake Tip-off

See data sheet #87 for a complete description.

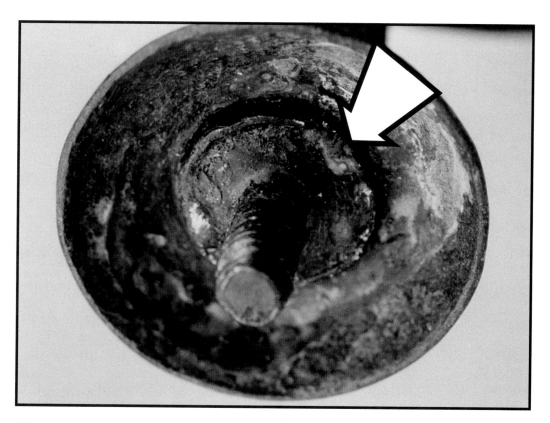

*Electric welding, a twentieth-century development, is shown here on the flanged stud assembly. Notice the modern machine-cut stud threads.*

# Tin Betty Lamp/Stand

## 91

This lighting device is a variant of the Ipswich Betty, a tin Betty lamp on a tidy or saucered tin stand. It is a complex assembly, made of many pieces of sheet metal soldered together. A nineteenth-century American design, its interesting shape will make a dramatic statement in colonial restorations.

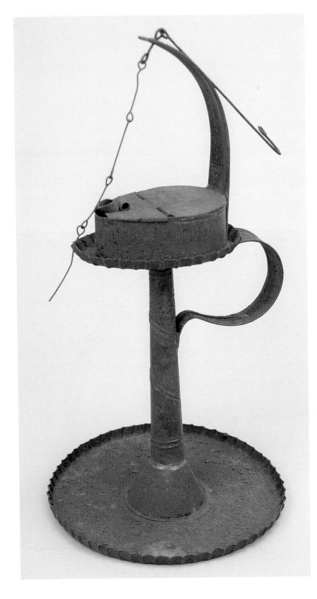

**Overall Height: 12 5/8"**
**Base Diameter: 6 3/4"**

Construction: The tidy, or stand, is constructed of .022" sheet steel, soldered to form an assembly 7 1/2" high. Both trays have irregular fluted edges. The Betty lamp is 3 3/4" long and 2 5/8" wide. The lamp bottom is made of heavier metal, with a rolled over and soldered seam. The soldered side seam is located under the offset hanger. An interesting feature of this fake is the duplication of the early factory fabrication feeling. The sheet metal has been cut clean and straight with none of the irregularities of hand fabrication.

Finish: The entire lamp assembly is given a special corrosive treatment that has produced a dusty rust finish. This duplicates what you might expect to see if this was found in the dirty confines of an old attic.

### Fake Tip-offs

**1.** Wear on the lamp font bottom and the stand surfaces is just not there. An authentically old device would have wear evident on all of those surfaces.

**2.** The overall appearance of this fake is too new to be authentic. There is no damage whatsoever to be found. There is no evidence of any grease or fat that would have been used for fuel. This is not a condition one would find on an old lamp.

*The symmetrically manufactured lines and excellent workmanship are evident in this view. The wick support is shown in its proper place, with a gap under the front edge to allow grease drips to return to the reservoir of the lamp.*

# Iron Betty Lamp

## 92

Betty lamps have been in use since the sixteenth century. Our pictured example, however, is an exception. It has been in use since 1992. Take a really close look at this one. It's beat up and rusty. How can you tell this is a "Fabulous Fake"? So much attention and care is paid to the manufacturing process that, on the surface, it is impossible to tell. In the paragraph that follows we will attempt to give you some pointers about this one's construction that should help with your future evaluations.

On a lighter note, no pun intended, it is a nice decorative accessory that in a pinch could be used as emergency lighting.

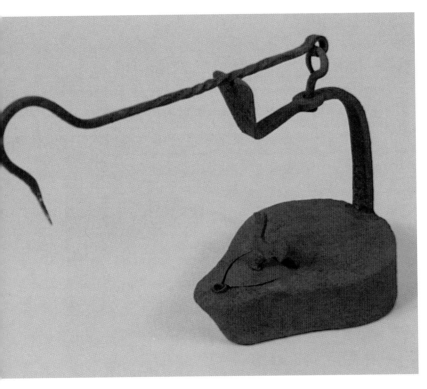

**Overall Height: 7 $^1/_{16}$" (less hanger)**
**Overall Width: 4 $^1/_4$"**
**Overall Length: 6 $^1/_4$"**

Construction: Let's start our review with the lamp font. It seems to be a three-piece fabrication, consisting of a top, side and bottom. All three are welded together with the square steel hanger support to form an oil-tight container. A thin sheet steel lid support is welded to the inside of the top cover. The sheet steel lid and hinge assembly is also welded to the inside of the top cover. The font height is 1 5/8". The 1/8" thick rooster knob adds another 1 1/2" in height to the font. The square hanger support rises vertically, bends to forms a mounting surface for the hanger rod and terminates in a flared hanger rod. The hanger rod is fabricated from square steel bar, twisted and forged into a large hook end. It is interesting that the hook is rod form and the shank is bar form.

Finish: An even amount of rust and corrosion pitting appears over the surface of the lamp. It looks like it has been hanging on a nail in an old barn somewhere, in a very damp climate. This Betty lamp can be a marvelous addition to your decorating scheme if purchased at the right price.

## Fake Tip-offs

**1.** Look at the font. On early lamps the bottom and sides would have been fabricated from one piece of sheet iron, hand-forged to shape. Certainly gas or electric welding was not available until the twentieth century.

**2.** Look at the hanger eye or loop. On the inside top surface of the eye loop, there should be evidence of a shallow wear groove if the lamp is an old one.

**3.** Look at the finish. The rusting and corrosion have evenly effected the entire surface of the lamp. Exposure like this is highly unlikely.

# Iron Pan Lamp

## 93

Here we have a re-created eighteenth-century or earlier pan or grease lamp design. Its simulated aged iron material and hand forged details seem to recall the smoky hardship of burning lard or oil. Today, however, they are used as decorative accessories in historic restorations.

Construction: At the top of the lamp is attached a boat-hook-shaped hanger rod. It is made of square steel rod with a twisted center section and hand-

forged ends. The hook end is bent back on itself and electric welded to a rounded point. Then the hook portion gently tapers to a point that is rolled over in a little curl. The pan lamp itself consists of three pieces of formed steel. The lamp pan is formed from sheet steel in a very irregular oval shape. The offset hanger support is formed from square stock, with the lower end welded to the pan. The other end is formed to provide a place for the attachment of the hanger eye and terminates in a flared hanger rest.

Finish: The pan lamp pictured here has been treated with a corrosive process to create the rusting and pitting of centuries. A final descaling to remove the heavy accumulation of rust leaves the lamp with a pitted silvery surface.

**Overall Height: 9 1/2"**
**(less hanger)**
**Overall Width: 5"**
**Overall Length: 5 3/4"**

*The hanger support weld to the pan mimics hand forging.*

**Fake Tip-off**

The hanger eye is about the only place that you can tell the difference between this re-creation and the real thing. On the inside top surface of the eye loop there should be evidence of a shallow wear groove if the lamp is an old one. If not... you know that what you have is likely a "Fabulous Fake".

# Iron/ Brass Sconce, Three Candle 94

An iron-looking metal frame rings the convex hand-hammered brass reflector of this medieval-looking three-arm wall sconce. The candle holders hook into a metal loop extending out from the curved surface of the reflector. Fastening to a wall is accomplished by a notched iron strap across the sconce back.

Equally at home in a contemporary or historical setting, these sconces are elegant.

Construction: A steel ring that looks like iron serves as the main frame for this sconce. Inserted in the ring is an oval convex brass reflector, fastened in place with five rivets. A steel strap hanger is riveted across the top of the reflector back, adding two more rivets to the fastening pattern. A steel loop, fastened to the back, extends through the reflector to the front, allowing the candle holders to hook on securely. The three twisted arms are welded together and finish ground to create the fastening hook. From the hook they arch gracefully out and are welded to the candle drip pans and tubes. Little curls of sheet steel are welded to the bottom of each arm.

Finish: The brass reflector is brightly polished. The steel pieces are given a corrosive treatment to obtain the look of rusting and corrosion pitting of a hand-forged iron look.

**Reflector Width: 11"**
**Reflector Height: 14"**
**Overall Depth: 9 3/4"**

### Fake Tip-off

The sconce arm hook and the mating reflector loop do not have any wear. They have sharp edges and the rough fit of a new assembly.

# Iron/ Brass Sconce, Three Candle    95

Ringed with a fake iron frame, the polished oval convex brass reflector is the same as the one shown on data sheet #94. The three-candle holder rod arms hook into a loop extending out from the curved front surface of the reflector. The cut and formed leaf style of the candle holders will lend an elegant touch to both contemporary and historical settings.

Construction: Three 5/16" diameter rods are welded together and finish ground to create the fastening hook. From the hook they arch gracefully out to meet the candle drip pans and tubes. Here the pans and tubes are welded in place. Decorative pieces of steel welded to each arm are the last details to be finished.

Finish: The hand-hammered brass reflector is brightly polished prior to assembly. The steel pieces are given a corrosive treatment to obtain the rusting and corrosion pitting needed to simulate a hand-forged iron finish.

**Reflector Width: 11"**
**Reflector Height: 14"**
**Overall Depth: 9 3/4"**

## Fake Tip-off

The sconce arm hook and the mating reflector loop do not have any wear. They have sharp edges and the rough fit of new assembly.

# Lighting Device Summary

In the illustration below a number of rush holders have been grouped together. It should be quite evident from the picture that there are differences between items of the same basic design. Most of these differences are purposely created to insure individuality and to make positive identification difficult. The rush holder jaws and the hinge are about the only common details. The bases, shanks and counterweight arms vary all over the lot. Even the overall height dimensions vary.

What you see here in the rush holders is also true for most of the other lighting devices shown in this section. Dimensions and material sizes may change, but there is one constant and that is the production techniques used. One good and sure way of comparing techniques is to have several "Fabulous Fakes" of your own to use as comparisons.

Finishes are also a variable that you have to watch out for. If a production lot was left in the corrosive treatment for too long, major material degradation is likely to occur. Some of the ball chandeliers are completely rusted through and have heavy scaling rust on the other parts. Other chandeliers have only light surface rust.

# V. Trade Signs

## Contents

**Overall Height: 21 1/2"**
**Hat Width: 9 1/2"**
**Hat Depth: 11 1/8"**
**Overall Depth: 13 1/4"**

# Top Hat Trade Sign 96

Haberdashers or hat merchants advertised their trade by displaying a tin replica of a hat outside their shops. The black iron-looking bracket and cheery orange top hat shown here represent a credible recreation of that early trade sign. The sheet metal hat slips onto an upturned bracket end and is held firmly by a sheet metal clip inside the brim. While the steel bracket makes no pretense about being old, the hat has an aged finish that is quite believable.

If you want to make a very dramatic decorating statement, this "Fabulous Fake" is a reasonable way to do it. Its not an original but it sure looks like it.

Construction: The top hat is fabricated from pieces of .022" thick sheet steel, hand formed to shape. Crimped seams and solder are used to assemble the pieces. The hat band is a separate piece of sheet metal, soldered in place with a formed wire buckle. The bracket uses sheet steel and bar, cut to size, for its handmade form. The pieces are riveted and welded together. The shoulder stop for the hat is a rectangular washer that has been welded in place and finish ground. The other end of that same bar has been shouldered, inserted through the back plate and welded over a flat washer, simulating a hand-forged rivet head. This is an attempt, though not a serious one, to simulate hand forging.

Finish: The bracket has been primed and has a finish coat of black paint applied. The tin top hat has also been primed, but the primer has had a cracking agent added to it. A top finish coat of orange and black has been applied. A dark colour glaze completes the manufacturing by highlighting the cracks in the undercoat.

## Fake Tip-off

The tin hat lacks the signs of rust that an antique outdoor sign would be expected to have. The painted finish of this fake evenly coats its tin form. The only wear evident is the finely scratched surface, resulting from a wire wool rubdown. No outdoor weather has ever touched its paint.

# Cocked Hat Trade Sign

Official headgear was advertised with a great flair by the use of this tin trade sign. Sweeping down from its crown and badge of rank are the pointed ends of the hat, terminated in gold braid. The badge of rank appears only on one side.

Mounting to the wall bracket has been accomplished by using a tubular socket welded to cross bracing inside the bottom of the hat. The socket, slipped over the upturned end of the wall bracket, makes a solid mounting. The bracket mounting allows the hat positioning to vary ninety degrees.

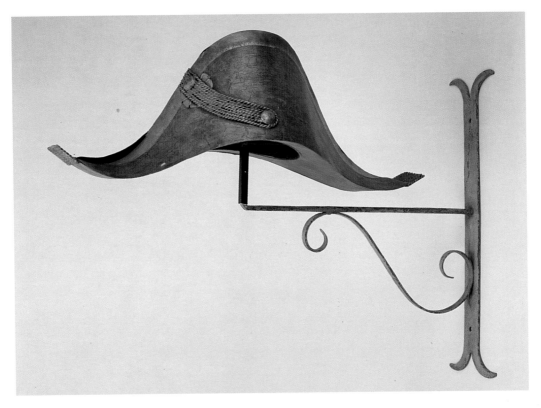

**Overall Height: 25 1/4"**
**Hat Width: 10 5/8"**

**Hat Length: 25 1/4"**
**Hat Height: 9 5/8"**

Construction: The assembly of the full-bodied hat is fabricated from sheet steel, using crimped and soldered seams. Twisted wire forms the braid at the hat points and the rank symbol on the side. The rest of the symbol details are formed from sheet steel and soldered in place. Cross bracing to hold the bracket socket is soldered to the bottom inside edge of the hat.

The bracket is made from steel sheet and bar, cut to size and hand formed. The pieces are riveted and electrically welded together. The hat mounting bar has one end bent at ninety degrees and the other shouldered. The shouldered end is inserted through a hole in the mounting back plate and welded over a flat washer to simulate a hand-forged head,

Finish: A primer coat of paint is applied directly over the sheet steel's mill surface (the finish of the metal as it comes from the producer). A special drier is added to the primer to create the cracked finish. A final coat of red is applied to the hat exterior and the braid details are painted gold. The hat is antiqued with a dark glaze to highlights its cracked finish.

**Fake Tip-offs**

**1.** The painted finish of this exterior sign has never been exposed to the weather. An authentically old sign should have rusted metal and some deterioration of the painted surface.

**2.** The mounting bracket would be a true hand-forged iron assembly, not an electrically welded modern steel fabrication.

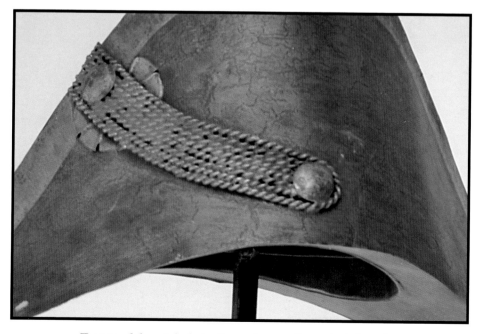

*Typical braid detail and rough paint finish.*

# Man in the Moon Trade Sign     98

Symbolic signs have always been eye catchers. The staring face of the man in the moon is no exception. The wide eyes, pointed nose and pursed lips of this tin trade sign, hanging outside a shop or office, would certainly get a passerby's attention. The sign has a swivel eye on its top edge that allows it to turn in the direction of the wind when hung outside. One enterprising modern artist, realizing the strength of its metal construction, hung one of the fakes outside for several years. The paint eventually peeled off. When its metal surface had completely rusted, he painted it in faded blue paint. You know the old saying... "Once in a blue moon".

Construction: The two sides of the moon are each hand hammered into form and are then trimmed to a finished form. The two sides are assembled with the swivel eye and soldered together. Facial details are highlighted and rough soldered seams are smoothed over, using a plastic body compound. A secondary tin nose end is soldered to the face and contoured into the main part of the moon, using plastic body compound. The moon's nose actually has nostrils.

**Overall Height: 15 3/4"**
**Width: 3"**
**Depth: 10"**

Finish: A heavy red primer has been applied to the entire outer surface. A finish top coat of color applied with subtle facial shading and feature details finishes the manufacturing process.

## Fake Tip-off

Plastic body compound is a twentieth-century development. The seams and joints would have been more noticeable on an original trade sign.

**Overall Height: 24"**
**Overall Width: 23"**
**Depth: 5"**

# Radiant Sun Trade Sign **99**

In the first part of the nineteenth century, an English fire insurance provider called The Sun Insurance Company adopted this as its symbol.

To make a sign that would stand up to the rigors of English weather, sheet steel was chosen as the main construction material. The sign was made three-dimensional, with a face on each side. The facial details were hammered out of tin and soldered in place. Steel hooks were crimped and soldered at the ends of two of the sun's rays, ninety degrees apart. These were hooked to a bracket mounted on their building.

A testimonial to the accuracy of the re-creation is the inclusion of this "Fabulous Fake" in some of the world's premier antique price guides.

Construction: A piece of sheet steel is hand formed in a mold to create a three-dimensional face. Two faces are made, trimmed to size, and their flanges soldered together. The rays of the sun are made separately and soldered to the sun's flange in an alternating pattern. At the point of attachment to the flange, plastic body compound has been used to make a smooth filler. Two mounting hooks are soldered to the arm's ends.

Finish: The metal surface has a mill finish with minor corrosion. Red primer, with a top finish coat of colors, is applied over it. The face detail painting finishes the manufacturing process.

**Fake Tip-off**

The original sign probably was made with the rays as an integral part of the body. Plastic fill certainly was not used in the nineteenth century. On this fake it has been used extensively. The light grey compound can be found by scratching at the base of the sun's rays.

# Spectacles Trade Sign 100

In the 1800's' it was a common sight to see tin trade signs like this wherever eyeglasses were sold. When the country antiques market developed, it was not long before antiques dealers and collectors had driven the price of original signs high enough to warrant the con artists of the world faking them.

Construction: Sheet steel is cut to size, hand formed and assembled with soldered crimped seams. The eye piece frames are a two-piece construction, with the soldered nose details connecting the two frames. Wire loops soldered on the top of each frame serve as hangers for the sign. The white center section of each frame is a thin sheet steel piece that is sandwiched between the frame halves.

Finish: The sign is constructed from aged or lightly rusted steel. Over this surface has been applied a primer coat along with the finish colors and detail painting. There is some chipped paint and scuffing that aids in the deception of its age.

### Fake Tip-offs

**1.** The use of red or brown primer is a sure indication of a fake sign. Look for areas with chipped paint. You will see the primer.

**2.** The steel rings used to hang the sign show no signs of wear. This is another bogus sign characteristic.

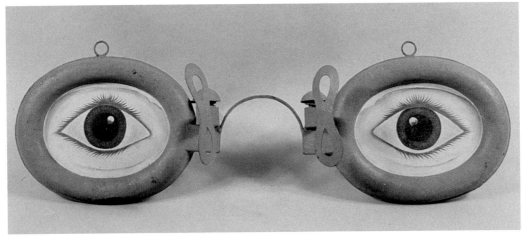

**Overall Height: 11"**
**Eye Length: 12 ³/₄"**

**Overall Width: 34 ³/₈"**
**Eye Height: 10"**

# Spectacles/ Banner Trade Sign   101

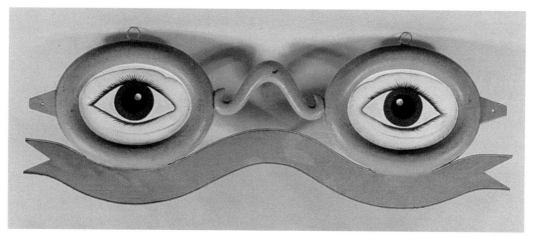

**Overall Height: 14"**
**Eye Frame Length: 13"**

**Overall Length: 38 3/4"**
**Eye Frame Width: 10"**

**Banner Width: 2 3/4"**

The original of this spectacles advertising must have really been something to see, with its reproduction copy so great. The three-dimensional eyeglass frame and flowing banner, along with an aged finish, make this copy almost believable as an original. An interesting feature of this sign is the fact that the flowing banner has not been painted with a name.

Construction: Sheet steel is cut to size, hand formed and assembled with soldered crimped seams. The eyeglass frames are a two-piece construction, with a three-dimensional nose bridge connecting them. Hanging loops, 1" in diameter, are soldered to the top of each frame. The white center section of each frame is a thin sheet that has been sandwiched between the frame halves.

The flowing banner has been cut from sheet steel, with sides rolled over wires to form smooth, rounded edges. Assembly of the banner has been accomplished by soldering it to the bottom flange of both frames.

Finish: The lightly rusted steel surface has been prime coated. Finish colors and detail painting have been applied over this semi-rough surface. This, along with some paint chipping, gives the sign an aged look.

**Fake Tip-off**

Advice for this sign is the same as that found on data sheet #100.

# Partridge Trade Sign 102

This free hanging metal frame suggests that this bird served as a pub sign or a similar use. The partridge has a single leg that slips over a pivot pin that is part of the surrounding framework. A hand-forged swivel hook at the top of the frame allows the sign to rotate 360 degrees.

**Overall Height: 28 1/4"**  **Overall Width: 26 7/8"**
**Bird Height: 15 5/8"**  **Bird Width: 7 1/2"**
**Bird Length: 15"**

Construction: Parts of the partridge are fabricated sheet steel, crimped and soldered together. The bird's single leg is a seamed and soldered steel tube. The bird's eyes are dimples in its steel head, so that they protrude out from the surface. The cosmetic filling of the joints and seams is done by using plastic body filler, though this is not noticeable without some exploratory scratching. The framework is made from steel strapping in a welded form, with metal curls as decoration.

Finish: A mild corrosive treatment is used to create a film of rust on the surface. Over this, a coat of red primer is applied, sometimes with a drying or cracking agent added. A final finish coating of paint is applied to match a real bird's basic coloration. The steel framework is corrosively treated and is left in a mildly rusted condition.

## Fake Tip-off
Plastic body filler is a modern invention of the last forty years. It would not have been used on an antique.

# White Rooster Trade Sign 103

Whether for a poultry shop or a pub, this white rooster, when presented in a folksy image, is eye catching. A profile head and tail are mounted on a full body, made entirely out of sheet steel. With a cracked finish, a few chips in the paint and a dent or two in the sheet metal, it looks like it's had a long life.

Construction: The rooster is fabricated from sheet steel with details that for the most part seem to be soldered together. The bird's body consists of two rounded, formed halves, with a flat curved back piece. The tail feathers are cut to size from a flat sheet of steel and soldered in place between two body halves. Each of the two long feathers in the tail has a wire support soldered in place along its entire length. The head is made from two pieces of sheet steel, cut to size and riveted together in two places through the comb. It has been formed and soldered in place over the upper end of the body.
A piece of formed tubing and a transition piece are soldered in place on the bottom of the rooster, to provide a means of mounting.

Finish; A corrosive treatment has produced a light film of rust over the metal surface. Over this rust a coat of primer with a surface cracking additive is applied. Over the cracked primer, a final coating of finish color is applied to match a rooster's basic coloring.

**Fake Tip-off**

The primer undercoat is cracked. The finish white is not. It is impossible to have the top coat not cracked. An antique would have the cracks through to the metal surface.

**Overall Height: 24 5/8"**
**Overall Length: 25 1/4"**
**Width: 3"**

# Trade Sign Summary

The fact that the signs were exposed to the weather hastened their demise. Thus the chance of running across a real sign is extremely remote. Pushed to new highs by collectors, the increased cost of an original has given rise to the production of fakes.

I received a frantic telephone call the other day. A man's pleading voice rang out from the phone, explaining that he had purchased several trade signs from a dealer and he was having second thoughts about their authenticity. Could I help him? I asked him to send me some pictures of these "antique" trade signs. After reviewing his photographs, I realized that the signs in question were clearly fakes that had been crudely repainted or colored to hide their identity as mass-produced reproductions.

Examine the photograph on the right closely. On the upper part of the eyeglass frame you will notice a pebbly or speckled surface. This has been caused by a pretreatment of the metal to create the rusted surface so necessary for the illusion of age. The finish, primer and paint have been applied over the rust, something that would never be done on an original trade sign.

The red primed surface can be seen clearly in the areas of chipped paint. This is a common practice of the fakers and never would have been used on bona fide antiques.

Be sure when you buy something like this you know what you're getting and you pay an appropriate price for it. The frantic caller lost a lot of money by paying a top price for what he thought were real antiques. In reality they were fakes.

*The pebbly condition of the paint is caused by pre-corroding the steel.*

# VI. Wall Spikes, Game Racks & Crowns

## Contents

# Iron Wall Spike

# 104

**Height: 7 3/8"**
**Width: 7 1/8"**
**Depth: 10"**

Wall spikes were used for hanging lamps, candles and other household items that required a single peg. The sharp end was hammered into mortar joints of stone walls and into wooden beams by hitting the end of the weld joint, where the hook and spike meet.

Construction: Thin pieces of steel sheet are cut to size and roll formed to create nesting arcs. One end of each piece is formed into a tight curl. Nine of these pieces are nested and welded together. The curled weldment, its mirror image and a center weldment with a bird silhouette are all welded together and finish ground. The hook and spike details are cut from steel bar and hammer forged to shape. A head is welded on one end of the hook. Finish grinding shapes the spike and hammer head. The curl weldments, spike and hook are welded together and finish ground to eliminate the telltale marks of its modern welding. A few hammer blows on the spike and hook weldments completes the illusion of hand forging.

Finish: A corrosive treatment gives its metal surface a centuries-old rusted look.

**Fake Tip-off**
Its head has no indication of ever being hit. If this spike were antique and had been used, its soft iron head would show a crushed or hammered-over surface.

# Wooden Birds Game Rack 105

Food in earlier years was handled and stored in a manner much different than today. Meat, in the form of game, poultry and small animals, was stored in a cool area or larder, hanging from sharp hooks high off the floor. Most often these hooks were mounted on their own boards or brackets and were quite decorative.

This one has its hooks mounted on a single green painted back board, scalloped on the top and carved with a bird on each end. The primitive character of this rack is reinforced by its hand-forged metal hooks and wooden back.

Construction: Two birds are hand carved on the 7/8" thick back board. Six holes are drilled through the board. The steel hook ends are inserted through the holes, then bent over and hammered flat.

Finish: The steel hooks are corrosively treated. The back board is artificially aged, with worn, rounded edges and a roughened surface. A heavy coat of cracked red primer has been applied along with a finish top coat of green paint.

**Fake Tip-off**
An uncracked top coat of paint pegs this rack as a fake. If the primer is cracked, the green paint should be cracked as well.

**Overall Length: 33 1/2"**     **Height: 7 3/4"**     **Depth Average: 2 5/8"**

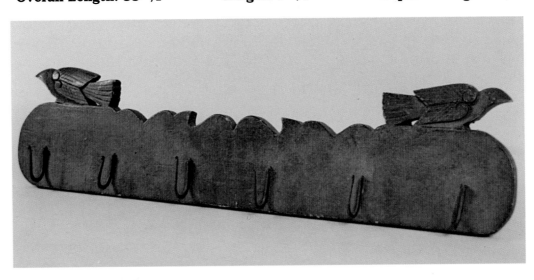

# Wooden Game Rack 106

Scandinavian-looking, with its heavily scrolled back board, this game rack indeed seems to be an eighteenth-century original. However, the truth be known, it was made just a few months ago, in a tropical country far from northern Europe.

It is a marvelously aged piece with great decorating potential. With nine hand-forged hooks, it could make a wonderful rack for drying flowers or herbs.

Construction: The scroll design and two rounded ends are hand cut on the 13/16" thick back board. Two 5/8" diameter mounting holes are drilled through the back board. Steel hooks inserted through the holes have their protruding ends hammered flat.

Finish: The hooks are corrosively treated to produce a rusty, aged surface. The back board is artificially aged, with worn rounded edges and a roughened surface. A heavy coat of cracked primer is finished with a top coat of green paint.

**Fake Tip-off**

The cracked red primer can be seen in the chipped areas of the back board. The primer is a fake give away with its uncracked top coat of green. On a real antique, the top coat would be cracked as well.

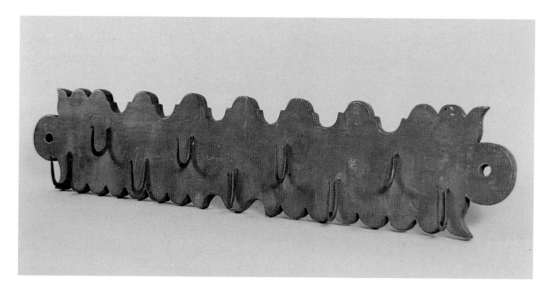

**Length: 34 ³/₄"**          **Width: 7 ¹/₈"**          **Depth Average: 2 ⁵/₈"**

# Scalloped Top Game Rack 107

Originally this rack hung in a pantry or larder, keeping meat and game out of the reach of pests and pets. In later years it kept kitchen utensils organized. Today it's used for hanging not only utensils but also dried flowers and herbs. This rack is not old. It is a re-creation, manufactured to replicate an original eighteenth-century game rack. It has a marvelous rusty finish and just the right amount of primitive iron-looking detail.

**Overall Height: 18 5/8"**
**Width: 24 1/8"**
**Depth: 2 1/4"**

Construction: The steel decorations consist of sheet steel curls, welded to a rectangular twisted center bar. The weld is finish ground flat for fitting to the back of the rack. Five blunt-pointed hooks are formed and riveted to the back along with the three decorative pieces. A 1/8" thick by 3/8" wide strip of steel is formed in a scalloped design and riveted to the rack back. Two 3/8" diameter hanging holes are punched through the ends of the 3/32" thick by 1 3/4" wide rack back.

Finish: The entire rack is given a corrosive treatment that produces an aged finish on the metal surface. The resulting rust and pitting have been left untouched.

### Fake Tip-offs

**1.** The 3/8" diameter hanging holes are perfectly round. On an authentic device they would not be perfectly round. Normal use would have distorted their shape.

**2.** Examine the weld areas of the decorative metal curls. You can see a build-up of material left by the modern welding process.

# Small Bird Game Rack                108

A bird silhouette in a nest of steel curls gives this game rack a nice decorative touch. Originally used for hanging provisions in an early Georgian larder, it is now used for hanging utensils in a country kitchen. Its crude workmanship and slightly banged up condition are deliberate techniques used to further the illusion of centuries of age.

**Overall Height: 9 3/4"**
**Width: 14"**
**Depth: 2"**

Construction: A sheet steel silhouette of a bird is welded to a piece of square steel bar. Four sheet steel curls are positioned around the bird and welded in place. The weldment end is finish ground flat for fitting to the back of the rack. The two fleurs-de-lis are assembled in the same fashion. A square steel bar is step formed for the hanger with its ends forged flat to fit the rack. The 1/8" thick by 1 1/4" wide strap steel back is fabricated with five rivet holes and five mounting holes for the forged steel hooks. The hooks are inserted through the holes in the rack and riveted in place. The remaining details are positioned in place and riveted. All the rivet heads are hammered and distorted to give the impression of centuries old construction.

Finish: The faker uses a corrosive treatment to obtain the rusted, aged look of the rack's surface.

## Fake Tip-off

The welding used on this rack is a twentieth-century development. Refer to Fake Tip-off #2 on the previous page.

# Four Bird Iron Game Rack

**Overall Height: 14 $^1/_8$"**
**Width: 24 $^3/_8$"**
**Depth: 2 $^7/_8$"**

The blunt points on the hooks indicate its probable use as a utensil rack as well as for hanging game. It is a sturdily built rack and would have stood up well to heavy storage weights.

The arcing back strap with the small loop at the top serves as the primary hanger. Secondary support is provided by fastening it to the wall, using the holes at either end of the rack. The back piece is offset to allow additional clearance for the four center hooks.
I can say unequivocally that this is one of the best game rack re-creations that I have ever seen. The aged finish is superb and lends credence to the illusion of age. The workmanship is excellent and close attention has been paid to even the smallest of details.

Construction; The decorative weldments are created by welding a steel bird silhouette to a square shank and four steel curls. Shaped steel hooks are then welded to the bird assemblies. The center weld joint is finish ground and hammered to look hand forged. The steel arched back serves as the center piece for the end weldments. Each end is welded to four steel curls and a steel hook. All of the hook assemblies are then riveted to the 3/32" thick by 1 3/4" wide back. Two 3/16" diameter mounting holes are drilled through the ends of the back piece. All the rivet headings are over-hammered and distorted to give the impression of centuries-old construction.

Finish: The entire rack is given a corrosive treatment that produces an aged finish on the metal surface. The rusted and pitted rack is then given a staining wax final coating to stabilize the finish and prevent further rusting.

## Fake Tip-offs

**1.** The construction of the hook assemblies on the original rack is done by hand forging. Modern welding is substituted on the fakes. This is evidenced by examining the sides of the hook to the curl joints. Notice the build-up left by the addition of the welding wire. This is a by-product of modern welding. Even though the the weld joint is finish ground, the end of the weld has not been removed.

**2.** The two drilled holes at the ends of the rack do not show any wear or distortion. There is no indication that this rack was ever mounted.

# Diamond Point Iron Game Rack 110

The condition of this rack might lead you to think that it had a hard life. The heavily rusted metal hooks, bent at all angles, and the crude fabrication lend credence to that thought. However, there is not a shred of truth to that picture of age. This game rack is a totally new piece. It has been artificially aged with a surface finish of rust that has eliminated all indications of modern manufacture. Even crude workmanship was encouraged to further the illusion. Going to all that trouble to produce a primitive-looking rack has paid off for those in the business of selling fakes.

**Overall Height: 12 ¹¹/₁₆"**     **Width: 21 ¹/₂"**     **Depth: 2"**

Construction: The decoration is made of sheet steel curls welded to a center twisted bar that is tipped with a forged diamond point. The weld is finish ground and hammered flat. Five hooks are hand forged with right angle tails. The 1/8" thick by 1 1/4" wide strap steel back is fabricated with five rivet holes and two 1/4" diameter punched mounting holes. The 5/16" diameter hanging rod is cut to size, formed to shape and fastened to the rack using the hook tails as rivets.

The remaining steel hooks are inserted through the rack back and forged, riveting them in place. All the rivet heading is over-hammered and distorted to give the impression of centuries-old construction.

Finish: The entire rack is given a corrosive treatment designed to create a surface finish that looks original. The resulting heavy corrosion virtually eliminates all the machine marks of modern manufacture.

**Fake Tip-offs**

**1.** The mounting holes at the rack ends do not show any signs of the wear or distortion that would have normally occurred as a result of its being mounted. The holes have been punched and rounded with burrs that indicate that modern manufacturing methods have been used.

**2.** The welding used in the assembly of the decorative pieces is a twentieth-century development. Reference data sheet #109.

### *Corrosion Results*
*This picture is worth a thousand words. Look at the surface rust and the feeling of age it imparts.*

# Harp Back Iron Game Rack     **111**

In a large house, one might find a number of these game racks hanging in the larder. A wall lined with these racks would be quite decorative. This graceful design has been executed with great success by today's fakers using modern manufacturing techniques. The cutting, shaping and welding has been done in a way that certainly looks eighteenth century and does not immediately give away its true age.

**Overall Height: 12 ³/4"**          **Width: 21 ¹/2"**          **Depth: 2"**

Construction: The decoratively formed steel of its back is made from pieces of sheet stock that are cut to size, formed and welded together. The lower ends of these are finish ground to simulate hand forging. The decorative pieces are riveted to the 3/32" thick by 1 1/4" wide back bar. Hand-forged steel hooks are inserted through the back bar and riveted in place. A 3/16" square piece of steel strap is cut to size, formed and riveted to the back bar. A 5/16" diameter hole is punched in each end of the back bar for hanging.

All the rivet heading is over-hammered and distorted, to give the impression of centuries-old construction.

Finish: The entire rack is corrosively treated to create the rusted surface one might expect to find on a rack of this type. The resulting finish effectively conceals all the machine marks of its modern manufacture.

### Fake Tip-offs

**1.** The mounting holes at either end of the rack exhibit no wear or distortion that would result from its being mounted. Also, The holes have been punched round with the material burrs that indicate modern methods have been used.

**2.** Look for additional material added to the forged-looking welds. That line or build-up is the telltale sign of modern electric welding.

*The exquisite design is highlighted in this close-up view. The metal's surface finish, created by the corrosive treatment, covers the telltale marks of modern manufacture.*

# Step Back Iron Game Rack 112

**Overall Height: 12 7/16"**      **Width: 21"**      **Depth: 2"**

Here is an example of a game rack that bears a striking resemblance to the diamond point rack on data sheet #110. Its crude form, bearing the telltale marks of a hard life, has been purposely manufactured this way. The stepped-back design and the fastening to the center decoration prohibit using the back as a means of hanging. This rack should be mounted using the holes located at either end of the rack bar. It is perfect for use as a utensil rack in a country primitive kitchen.

Construction: The decoration is made of sheet steel curls, welded to a center twisted piece of sheet steel that is fastened to the stepped back.The weld is finish ground to a forged-looking shape. Five steel hooks are hand forged with right angle tails. The 1/8" thick by 1 1/4" wide strap steel rack back is fabricated with five rivet holes and two 1/4" diameter punched mounting holes. The 5/16" diameter rod back is cut to size, formed to shape and riveted to the rack back using two hook tails.
The remaining hooks are inserted through the rack back and forge riveted in place. All the rivet heading is over-hammered and distorted to give the impression of centuries-old construction.

Finish; The complete rack is given a faux finish that creates an illusion of great age. It is a corrosive treatment that rusts the metal surface in much the same way that exposure to the atmosphere would over a long period of time.

## Fake Tip-offs

**1.** There is again a noticeable lack of wear around the mounting holes in the rack back. The holes have been punched round with the material burrs that indicate modern manufacturing methods have been used. If this were a truly old rack, the holes would show signs of use.

**2.** Modern electric welding is used to assemble the decorative metal curls. Examine the joint closely for traces of extra weld material and signs of finish grinding.

# Iron Game Crown

The beauty of a simple form has been a basis of good design for centuries. The game crown shown here embodies that form. The simple framework supports nine hooks. Old rusted metal, hand forged and riveted together, makes an authentic-looking re-creation. Its a great device for drying herbs and flowers or hanging utensils. These fakes can be found as a standard stock item in many antique shops.

**Overall Diameter: 14 1/8"**
**Overall Height: 10"**

Construction: A piece of sheet steel, 3/32" thick by 1 1/2" wide is rolled into a circle and riveted closed. Three square steel bars are bent into a crown frame and are welded together at the top. A hanging loop is added to the top and welded in place. Finish grinding blends all the welds to simulate hand forging. The lower ends of the crown members are forged flat and riveted to the inside of the circular band. Nine sharp pointed steel hooks are hand forged and riveted to the outside of the frame.

Finish: The complete game rack is given a corrosive treatment that produces the centuries-old look that you see here.

## Fake Tip-off

The hanging loop has no wear on the inside top surface. An old crown would show some evidence of its age and use by a deformed surface.

# Iron Bird Game Crown                    **114**

**Overall Diameter: 15 3/4"**
**Overall Height: 14 1/4"**

A game crown is designed to hang from the ceiling, with the game and meat hanging from its hooks, far above the hungry jaws of rodents and household pets. What you are looking at in this picture is a great form, reproduced to look like hand wrought iron. It is a game rack with bold little birds cut from sheet metal, nesting in what looks to be hand wrought curls of iron.

As you will see, everything is not really as it appears. Modern technology has eliminated many of the time-consuming methods employed in past centuries. Now electric and gas welding methods of fastening have replaced forge welding.

Still, even with the modern methods used, a good hand-forged appearance has been obtained. The rusted, aged look of this rack is sure to fool many an antiques buff as it did the folks in the October 1991 issue of Early American Life. They purchased one of the bird game crowns. It highlighted their collection of early iron and was identified as a northern European form of the late eighteenth century.

Construction: Four bird silhouettes are cut from sheet steel and are welded to a square bar to form the hooks. Steel curls are cut and formed. Four are welded to each of the square bar hooks. They are finish ground flat to simulate hand forging. A 3/32" by 1 1/2" sheet steel band is rolled into shape and rivet fastened. The crown is formed from four 1/4" square steel hook bars that rise above the band and are bent to meet in the center, where they are welded together. A forged hook is added to the top for hanging. All the weldment details are riveted to the circular iron band. One true bit of hand forging is the small section of twist in each leg of the crown assembly.

Finish: The entire game crown assembly has been given a corrosive treatment that leaves its surface with a rusted finish that really looks ancient.

## Fake Tip-offs

**1.** The joint that bonds the curls to the bird and hook should be looked at closely. An authentic, old hand-forged weld will not exhibit a material build-up at the joint edges. Reference data sheet #109, Fake Tip-off #1.

**2.** The inside of the hanging loop shows no wear. An eighteenth-century piece will show considerable evidence of use-induced wear.

# Spikes, Racks & Crowns Summary

Their quality of reproduction is of the highest grade. The fakers that produced the spikes, racks and crowns shown in this chapter have done their homework. They have taken popular old designs and, using modern manufacturing techniques, are producing them in substantial quantities.

Their products are as accurate in design and finish as the eighteenth-century originals. As soon as you think you have a particular item figured out as a fake, with all the material sizes, dimensions and finish noted, the crafty producers change everything. They change the material sizes. Thicker or thinner, it makes no difference to them as long as they can still beat it with a hammer or electric weld it. Overall sizes are not fixed. They can make a product bigger, smaller or in a whole range of sizes. They can change one dimension or all of them.

Finishes are not locked in either. Plain steel can be treated for no rust, a light film, or even a heavy scaling rust with severe surface pitting. A waxy stabilizer coating may or may not be applied. Some items are painted, some are not.

A "Fabulous Fake" is a tough product to identify. It has been made purposely to resemble the original item as much as is economically possible. There are, however, several things you can look for that will help you in your evaluation of a piece:

    1. Examine the form. Does it match any illustrated in this book?

    2. Examine the mounting holes for wear, distortion and proper burr removal.

    3. Look for modern weld undercutting and weld pooling of metal.

Its all right to buy a piece, whether it's fake or real, as long as you pay the appropriate price.

### Modern Factory
*The welding and grinding used on the fakes in this chapter is done using twentieth-century equipment.*

# VII. Tin Birds & Decoys

## Contents

# Stork Roof Finial

In Holland, good fortune is symbolized by the stork. The birds have been encouraged to nest on buildings, with the owners perhaps hoping for more than bird droppings.

Many building owners, tired of the storks' large, messy nests of twigs and sticks, opted for tin replicas instead. So the European white stork was created in painted tin as a full size, real-looking bird in a roof finial form. The three-legged stand shown in the illustration is used for display purposes only and is not part of the finial. The stork was normally mounted on the gabled roof end on an iron bracket and allowed to pivot in the wind.

It is amazing the amount of detail that is put into the manufacture of this replica. The form of the body and legs is very accurate and close to a full-scale duplication. Combined with a colorful, detailed paint finish, our European white stork finial is a great decorating idea.

**Overall Height: 36 1/4"**
**Overall Length: 32"**
**Width: 6"**

Construction: The stork and finial are fabricated from steel sheet, steel tubing and turned details. The steel tubing and turned pieces are welded together to form the basic standing leg and finial. The stork body has been assembled from sheet steel parts, tack welded, crimped and soldered together.

Some cosmetic filling of joints and seams has been done using plastic body filler.

Finish: The exterior of the stork has been given a corrosive finish, designed to create a light film of rust on the metal surface. Over this rust a coat of red primer has been applied. In some cases it has a drying or cracking agent added to it. The final paint coating is applied to match the real stork's coloration.

**Fake Tip-Offs**

**1.** Look inside the open end of the leg. You will see a twentieth-century seamless steel tubing. Early tubing would have crimped or soldered seams.

**2.** Red primer is a modern production technique. That would not be found on an antique bird.

**3.** If you are able to discreetly scratch one of the fillet areas, plastic body filler will be uncovered. It is a true indication of a fake.

*The excellent quality of the painted finish is evident in this close-up of the leg structure.*

# Partridge Decoy 116

The European chukar partridge has been immortalized in the tin form of the decoy that you see here. It is thought that decoys were used in an attempt to draw partridges out into the open where they would be easy prey for hunters. The decoy originally stood in the field on two tubular legs that could be pushed into the ground with the tail serving as an additional brace.

The third tube, on the birds underside, is actually a mouthpiece for a whistle that emits sound from a screened opening under the decoy's beak.

As you can see from the illustration here, the condition of the decoys can vary. On some you will find the painted surface to be in good condition. On others there is heavy rust and scaling paint. Someone has even come up with the idea of adding feet to the decoys, though that is somewhat doubtful as an original accessory.

These partridge decoys have been sold as originals for years. They have fooled dealers and collectors all over the world.

**Overall Height: 8 1/8"**     **Overall Length: 8 3/8"**     **Width: 3 5/8"**

Construction: The partridge has been fabricated from thin sheet steel in detail parts that are crimped and soldered together. The legs and the whistle are seamed and soldered 9/32" diameter steel tubes. A screen mesh, with 1/16" square openings, has been soldered in place to cover the whistle opening.

The cosmetic filling of the joints and seams is done with plastic body filler, though this is not noticeable without some exploratory scratching of the painted surface.

The bird's eye is dimpled in the material, so that it protrudes from the surface of the head.

Finish: The exterior surface of the bird is corrosively treated, to produce a film of rust. Over this rust, a coat of red primer is applied. In some cases a drying and cracking agent is added. The final coating of finish is applied to match the real bird's basic coloration.

## Fake Tip-off

**1.** The painted surface of the bird has noticeable small bubbles on its surface. These are the result of paint being applied over the rusted steel. Rust does not really happen that way on tin. You will notice that when bits of paint chip off, the surface is already rusted. That condition would not occur on an original decoy.

**2.** Plastic body filler is a post-World War II development. It would not have been used on an antique.

*The feet are not original but they look it.*

# European Duck Decoy                    117

Copied from the style of a European decoy, this little fellow is but one of an almost endless variety of fake duck decoys. The colors and shapes available are as endless as the imagination of the craftsmen that make them. The carved feather detail and authentic-looking colors, combined with an aged finish, give these birds a natural woodlands accent.

Construction: The body is made from one piece of wood, with the wing tips and tail feathers carved in relief. The head and neck are carved from one piece of wood with dowel reinforcement in the neck. The finish filler around the base of the neck is made from grey plastic body filler and blended into a smooth contour. The bottom of the duck's body is left basically unfinished, with the end of the neck dowel visible.

Finish: The wood surface of the bird has been left with some visible tool marks and rough grain. Over this has been applied a heavy coating of red primer. It appears that the primer has been sanded to provide a semi-smooth surface for the finish coat of color.

**Fake Tip-off**

Grey plastic body filler is a modern development and would not be found on a decoy made before World War II.

**Overall Height: 6"**
**Overall Length: 14"**
**Width: 5"**

# Swan Decoy

Is it a Trumpeter or Whistling Swan? They are so similar that, when reproduced in a primitive or folksy form, as shown here, you cannot tell which one it is. Ours is hand crafted out of native Indonesian wood and finished in a worn, cracked white paint with lots of red primer showing through. When you see it for the first time, you might think, due to the weathered surface of the decoy, it has had a hard life in the field. The distressed condition of its painted surface has created the same effect on the wood that rust has for the steel pieces shown in other chapters. An aura of considerable age has been instantly developed.

Construction: The bird's body is constructed from three boards that have been glued together. They have been rough cut to the proper outline and then hand shaped to the final form. The arched

Overall Height: 19 3/4"
Overall Length: 37"
Width: 11 1/2"

neck, cut from one piece of wood, is glued to the head. Hand carving is used to attain the final head, beak and eye detail.
Grey plastic body filler has been used to make the necessary neck to body fillers.

Finish: The swan is sanded smooth and all the contours blended evenly. A rough, cross-brushed coat of red primer with a cracking agent is the base for the finish colors. The final white paint with black details is brushed on over the intentionally rough surface. In order to further the illusion of age, much of the finish paint has been removed using wire wool, exposing the red undercoat of primer.

**Fake Tip-offs**

**1.** Grey plastic body filler is a twentieth-century invention. A truly old decoy would not have used this type of product.

**2.** The cracked red primer is a fake giveaway. The top coat of paint should be cracked; it is not.

# Sandpiper Decoy **119**

The soft brown plumage of this shore bird leads one to think that it is related to the sandpiper family. The wings are carved in relief on the body sides. Its aged and cracking finish could give credibility to a claim of years of use. The base makes no pretense of being old. This makes sense, because originally a decoy was used in the field or at the shore, not on a bookcase shelf. Bases were added when people started collecting decoys and needed a display stand.

Construction: The body of the bird is carved from one piece of wood. The round head and neck is one piece, with the long beak doweled in place through the center of the head. The neck filler is made from grey plastic body filler and blended to a smooth contour. Wings of the bird are carved into the sides of the body and taper back to terminate at the tail. The base is a round wood turning with an iron tapered rod.

Finish: This shore bird has been given an overall coat of red primer, with a cracking agent added to it. Then the soft shades of brown and white finish paint are applied. The details are trimmed in contrasting colors of black, white, a little orange, and olive drab for the beak.

**Fake Tip-offs**

**1.** The hole drilled in the bird's underside is new and shows no evidence of age.

**2.** The plastic body filler is a post-World War II development.

**Overall Height: 14 1/2"**
**(including base)**
**Overall Length: 15"**
**Width: 3 1/2"**

# Tin Birds & Decoys Summary

There are hundreds of ways that unscrupulous people try to make a financial windfall by passing fakes off as real antiques, At a recent high stakes auction, I saw a European chukar partridge, waiting to be sold, next to a real antique decoy. Someone actually bought the partridge for five times its real value.

Be an informed buyer. Know the form of an antique that you are interested in buying. Whether you are collecting or just buying for the decorative value, learn how much you should pay for a fake. If you are only buying authentic antiques, you will be a step ahead in avoiding disappointment.

*A chukar partridge waiting to be sold.*

# VIII. Trammels & Gridirons

## Contents

# Basic Gridiron        **120**

The basic design of this gridiron is directed toward function. No thought was given to adding decorative frills or curls. Only what was needed to accomplish its primary function of cooking food was manufactured.

The simple grid is held over the glowing hot coals of a cooking fire by its three legs. The long handle provides a measure of isolation from the heat of the fire. The loop formed at the end of the handle is a means of hanging when not in use.

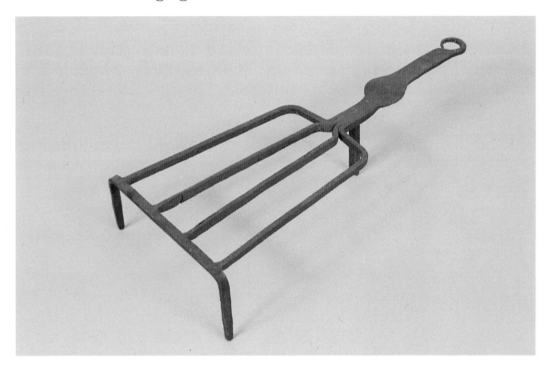

**Overall Length: 19 1/8"**      **Overall Width:8"**      **Height: 3 1/2"**

Construction: Though the original gridiron was made from two major pieces, our copy is assembled from many small steel components welded together to simulate the two hand-forged pieces. For example, the handle looks like it was slit to form the four grid bars. In fact, the handle detail is cut to size and butt welded electrically to the four preformed ends of the grid bars. The original piece probably had been made as one unit or forge welded from parts in a manner similar to our electrically welded assembly. Across the open ends of the grid bars, preformed front legs are electrically welded in place. The third leg is inserted through a hole in the handle and welded in place. All the welding is done in a way that simulates hand forging. In order to heighten the feeling of great age, the two center grid bars are made to look as though their iron material has delaminated from the effects of heavy use and the corrosion of centuries. Electric welding again has made this age deception possible. All indications of its modern manufacture are removed by finish grinding with a fine grit wheel and some minor cosmetic hammering.

Finish: The gridiron is given a corrosive treatment. This results in a rusted and pitted surface finish that one would expect to find on a seventeenth-century piece. A final dark wax finish is applied to create the luster of a treasured antique.

*The rusting and pitting of corrosion can clearly be seen.*

## Fake Tip-offs

**1.** Where the four grid bars meet the handle, the weld line of added steel from the automatic weld process can be seen.

**2.** There is no wear evident on any part of the gridiron. There should be some sign of wear on the inside of the handle loop and on the bottoms of the legs.

# Rectangular Gridiron 121

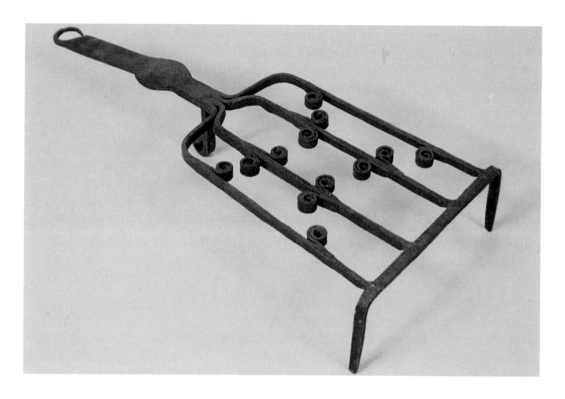

**Overall Length: 19 ¹/₂"**     **Overall Width: 8 ³/₄"**     **Height: 3 ³/₈"**

During the seventeenth and eighteenth centuries, gridirons were used for cooking food in an open fireplace. On a fireplace hearth it would not have been unusual to see several examples of this type, much in the same way that pots and pans would be seen in today's kitchen.

Construction: Though the original gridiron was made from two major components, this one has been assembled from many small steel pieces welded together to simulate the two hand-forged pieces. For example, the handle looks like it has been split to form the four grid bars. In fact, the handle detail has been cut to size and butt welded electrically to the four preformed ends of the grid bars. The original piece had probably been made as one unit or forge welded from details in a manner similar to our electrically welded assembly.

Across the open ends of the gird bars, preformed front legs are electrically welded in place. The third leg is inserted through a hole in the handle and welded in place. All the welding is done in a way that simulates hand forging. Twelve curling steel tendrils are electrically welded to the insides of the grid bars. In order to heighten the feeling of great age, the two center grid bars are made to look as though their iron has delaminated from the effects of heavy use and the corrosion of centuries. Electric welding again has made this age deception possible.

A finish grinding with a fine grit wheel and some minor cosmetic hammering remove all indications of its modern manufacture.

Finish: The brightly ground finish is removed with a corrosive treatment that leaves the steel surface with the rust and pitting that one would expect to find on a seventeenth-century antique. A final dark wax coating is sometimes applied to create the luster of polished iron.

### Fake Tip-offs

**1.** Where the curled tendrils meet the bars of the grid on a real antique there should be a faint line of the material joint gradually fading into the bond of the forge weldment. On fakes, the electric welding process used has melted both the tendril and the bar together plus adding additional the steel of the welding wire. The result is a solid joint with no material line of the detail parts.

**2.** There is no evidence of wear on the bottoms of the legs or on the inside of the handle loop.

**Fake Iron**
*The delamination of the two center grid bars is clearly shown in this picture. The iron curls show a connecting weld that is perhaps too consistent for a forged joint.*

# Heart Gridiron 122

Curling iron tendrils and beautiful open hearts distinguish this gridiron from its plainer cousins. The simulated hand forging has been well done and the surface treatment of the metal seemingly lends credence to its claim of antiquity .

Construction: Modern mild steel is the material of choice for the fakers as a replacement for wrought iron. Electric welding replaces the forge welding used on antiques.

The four outside bars of the grid are cut to length and formed to the designed shape. Two steel curls are welded in place on each outside grid bar. The center bar is welded together from preformed pieces. The five bars and two additional curls are butt welded to the knife blade handle. The preformed front legs are welded across the front of the five grid bars. The third leg is inserted through a hole in the butt weld area and welded in place.

In order to achieve the illusion of seventeenth-century creation, the two plain metal grid bars have been manufactured to look like they delaminated from the effects of heavy use and centuries of corrosion. Electric welding has made this age deception possible.

The weld areas are ground to a taper, using a fine grit grinding wheel. This and a little cosmetic hammering remove all indications of modern manufacture.

**Overall Length: 19 $^{11}/_{16}$"**
**Overall Width: 9 $^{1}/_{2}$"**
**Height: 2"**

Finish: The entire gridiron is given a corrosive treatment. As a result of this, the metal surface takes on a rusted and pitted appearance. A final coating of dark wax is sometimes applied to create the luster of polished iron.

### Fake Tip-offs

**1.** The lack of wear is one of the easiest indicators of modern manufacture to see. The curled metal rear leg on this gridiron, if it really were old, would have substantial flat wear on its bottom as a result of being scraped across the hearth bricks of many fireplaces. As you can see in this photograph, the bottom surface is just like new.

**2.** Electric welding is a process that adds metal to a joint. This can be seen as the rounded fillets on the inside of the grid bars where they join the front leg bar. The added material line can also be seen at the grid's points. A detail of a typical material line is shown on data sheet #109.

*The lack of wear is evident on the back foot. Look at the seventeenth-century corrosion simulation on the handle.*

# Four Heart Gridiron          **123**

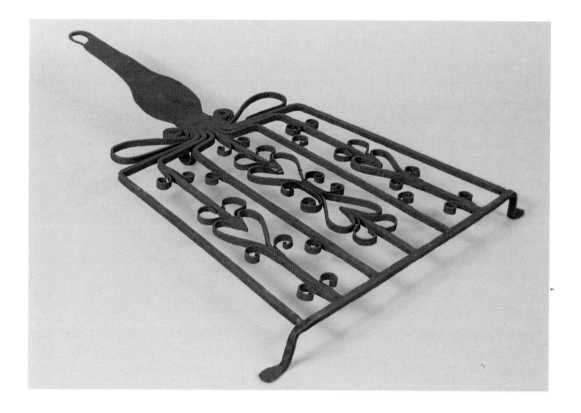

**Overall Length: 26 7/8"**                    **Overall Width: 18 1/2"**

**Height: 5"**
**(to the top of the offset handle)**

This gridiron has a decidedly French influence, with its well-defined grid pattern of large open hearts and tight curls of iron. Another interesting feature of this kitchen cooker is the offset handle. Its raised height was designed to keep fingers away from the hot coals of the cooking fire.

There is a striking similarity in our gridiron's seventeenth-century handle shape to the knife blade andirons of the eighteenth-century.

Construction; Four plain grid bars are formed and cut to size from steel bar. The three decorative bars with hearts and curls are then assembled by electric welding from precut and formed steel details. Two of the plain bars have two metal curls each, welded in place. The seven grid bars are electrically butt welded together at the handle end and trimmed to size. The front leg bar formed from steel bar stock is electrically welded across the open ends of the seven grid bars. Two curling steel tendrils are electrically welded in place on each side of the handle end of the grid assembly.

The sheet steel handle is then cut to size and electrically welded to the end of the grid assembly. The third leg is inserted through a hole in the handle and electrically welded in place.

All the welds are then finish ground using a fine grit wheel and cosmetically hammered to eliminate all the marks of modern manufacture.

Finish: The entire gridiron is given a corrosive treatment that gives the metal surface a rusted and pitted appearance. Often you will find a dark wax finish has been applied.

## Fake Tip-offs

**1.** The extra material from the wire feed electric welding can be seen where the handle meets all the grid bars and decorative curls. The faker's finish grinding has not completely removed the line of melted weld metal. This same condition can be seen in the center of the grid where the metal curls are welded to the bars.

**2.** The three feet of the gridiron show the clear definition of an "as manufactured" condition of the metal. On a true antique, there would be a flat area worn on the bottom of each foot brought about by the scraping action of a fireplace hearth.

*The ancient look of the surface is very apparent in this view.*

# Turned Handle Gridiron 124

Though it is one of the largest of its type, this gridiron is best characterized by its long solid handle, an unusual feature. Flat sheet iron was less expensive, easier to fabricate and did not allow as much heat build-up in the handle. With that in mind, the decision to use a solid round material might have been for esthetic rather than utilitarian reasons.

Construction: All seven grid bars are formed and cut to size. The outer bars are fabricated from solid steel bar stock. The inner grid bars are fabricated from sheet steel of varied thicknesses and fastened together by electric welding. They are welded intermittently so that, when rusted, the impression is that the iron has been delaminated from age and use. The decorative metal curls are then electrically welded to the inside of the grid framework.

The seven grid bars are electrically welded together at the handle end. The open end is welded to a preformed front leg bar. The solid turned handle, with an offset piece welded in place, is joined to the grid bar assembly by electric welding. The last two metal curls are welded in place, one on each side of the handle. The third leg is

**Overall Length: 31"**          **Overall Width: 16 7/8"**
**Height: 4 1/4"**
**(to the top of the offset handle)**

inserted through a hole in the handle and welded in place. Finish grinding with a fine grit wheel and cosmetic hammering remove all the marks of its modern manufacture.

Finish: The entire gridiron is given a corrosive treatment to give the metal surface a rusted, pitted look. It is finished with a final dark wax coating.

## Fake Tip-offs

**1.** Where the grid bars meet the front leg bar, you can see a fillet of weld material on the inside edges of the bars. On a true hand-forged joint, there would be no fillet and there would be no indication of welded material.

**2.** Again look for wear on the bottoms of the three feet. There is none. This is a clear indication of a fake.

# Wavy Round Gridiron                                125

This revolving round grid is a form of gridiron that is commonly found on the east coast of the United States. The alternating wavy and straight lines of this grid can provide a very distinctive decorating touch to a colonial setting. The revolving grid, slightly oval in shape, is pitched a little towards the fire due to its two shorter front legs. The handle is offset to provide more distance between the heat of the hearth and the cook's fingers.

Construction:
The revolving grid frame is fabricated from 1/16" thick by 3/4" wide steel strapping.. It is roll formed and electrically welded into its oval shape. The 1/16" thick, 1/4" wide wavy steel grid bars are formed, cut to size and welded in place. The three 1/16" thick flat steel grid bars are then assembled in the same fashion.
The front leg frame is cut to size from steel strapping, formed to shape and electrically welded to a preformed steel handle piece. The back leg, made from steel strapping and inserted through a hole in the handle, is welded in place.

**Overall Length: 24 ³/₄"**
**Grid Size: 13 " x 14"**
**Grid Height: 3 ³/₄"**
**(at front edge)**

The revolving grid is fastened to the leg and handle piece with a pivot pin welded to the leg frame.
Finish grinding and some cosmetic hammering used on the electric welds removes all indication of modern manufacture and furthers the illusion of hand forging.

Finish: The metal surface of this piece is treated with a corrosive process that prematurely ages it. A final wax coating prevents further rusting and gives the metal the luster of a restored antique.

## Fake Tip-offs

**1.** The grid bars show definite electric welding with the flow of the melted metal seen as fillets at the joint sides.

**2.** The center pin of the revolving grid does not exhibit the amount of wear one would expect on a device that is truly old. Its snug fit allows the grid to rotate smoothly, another indication of modern birth.

**3.** Examine the bottoms of the three feet. Flat areas worn on those surfaces would be normal for an antique. There are none on the fakes.

*This view of the handle shows the aged finish.*

# Pinwheel Gridiron                    126

The decorative appearance of this gridiron mimics a pinwheel, with its curved grid bars and revolving platform. It was a popular design in the early eighteenth century, probably due to its sturdy design and ability to provide a stable cooking surface. The handle at the circular center section is offset, providing more clearance between the hearth and the cook's fingers.

**Overall Length: 26 1/4"**
**Grid Size: 12 1/8" Diameter**
**Grid Height: 4 1/4"**

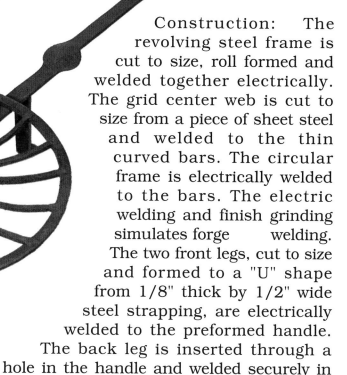

Construction: The revolving steel frame is cut to size, roll formed and welded together electrically. The grid center web is cut to size from a piece of sheet steel and welded to the thin curved bars. The circular frame is electrically welded to the bars. The electric welding and finish grinding simulates forge welding. The two front legs, cut to size and formed to a "U" shape from 1/8" thick by 1/2" wide steel strapping, are electrically welded to the preformed handle. The back leg is inserted through a hole in the handle and welded securely in place. The revolving grid is fastened to the leg assembly with a fixed pivot pin and welded in place. A detailed finish grinding of the electric weld areas, followed by some cosmetic hammering, virtually eliminates any indication of modern manufacture.

Finish: Aging of the gridirons is accomplished by using a corrosive process that gives the metal surface the rust and pitting characteristics of a true eighteenth-century piece. A final wax coating is sometimes used to stabilize the finish and give it the look of a fully restored antique.

### Fake Tip-offs

**1.** The center of the grid shows the trace of electric welding as a slight undercut where the grid bar meets the center hub. That undercut is caused by the burn-through of melted welding wire.

**2.** The outer ring shows the grid bars with a simulated hand-forged weld. To accomplish this appearance, the bar welds are ground to a feather edge that also removes some of the outer ring material. This material removal is not a condition consistent with hand forging. Forge welding requires repeated hammer blows and material heats to effectively weld. The constant localized working of the metal would tend to widen and flatten the material of the ring, not remove it.

**3.** Wear is a significant sign of old age. Flat areas should be worn on the bottoms of the three feet. The grid center pin should be worn, resulting in a loose fit. Lack of wear is a good indication your piece is a fake.

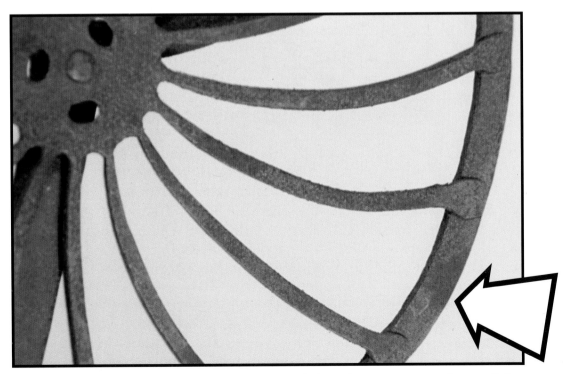

*The irregular outside diameter caused by clean-up grinding of the electric welding can be seen clearly.*

# Fleur-de-Lis Gridiron                    **127**

The interesting design of this gridiron or broiler, as it has sometimes been called, looks very practical. There are no large open areas where food, if it was cooked directly upon the iron grid, could fall through to the dirty hearth.

A French country influence is suggested by the cut sheet iron double fleur-de-lis of the revolving grid. The simulated hand forging and superbly aged finish are signature characteristics of this group of fakers.

Construction: The revolving grid frame steel material is cut to size, roll formed and electrically welded together. The grid center web is cut from a piece of sheet steel and welded to four thin members that reach out to the circular frame. Then they are electrically welded in place. The angular grid bars and the fleur-de-lis are cut to size from steel sheet and electrically welded to the circular frame.

The two front legs, cut to size and formed to a "U" shape from 1/8" thick by 1/2" wide steel strapping, are welded to the preformed, steel sheet handle. The back leg, inserted through a hole in the handle, is electrically welded in place. The revolving grid has been fastened to the leg assembly with a fixed pivot pin, welded in place. A detailed finish grinding of the electric weld areas, followed by some minor cosmetic hammering, virtually eliminates any indication of modern manufacture.

**Overall Length: 26 $^3/_4$"**
**Grid Size: 12 $^5/_8$"**
**Grid Height: 4 $^1/_4$"**

Finish: The metal surface of this piece is treated with a corrosive process that prematurely ages it. A final wax coating is sometimes applied to prevent further rusting and gives the metal the luster of a fully restored antique.

## Fake Tip-offs

**1.** On this gridiron, marks of modern machinery can be seen on the grid hub. After the electric welding operation, the excess weld material is removed with an electric grinder. Some of the marks of the modern grinding wheel have not been totally removed and can be seen as indentations on the metal surface.

**2.** The center pivot pin warrants close examination on this gridiron. The joint is tight with no appreciable play. On a truly old gridiron that has seen years of use there would be considerable wear, resulting in a loose fit.

**3.** The bottoms of the three feet do not exhibit the wear one should expect to find on a true antique.

*The round head of the pivot pin can clearly be seen in this close-up.*

# Decorated Trammel

# 128

In colonial times there was no way to effectively control the burning and heat of a fire. So a mechanical method was devised to raise or lower the pots, to control the amount of heat that food would receive.

The operation of this complex looking gadget, called a trammel, was relatively simple. The entire assembly was carried to the fireplace by lifting it by the bird's head handle on the left hand side of the trammel and holding the large ring at the top. The large ring was held up inside the top of the fireplace by an iron support bar. The trammel could then be adjusted by grasping the two levers on the right hand side. The top lever was lifted and the bottom lever was allowed to move to a new setting. Last, but not least, the cooking pot handle was slipped over the broad hook at the bottom of the trammel.

The metal construction of our "Fabulous Fake" has been faithfully copied from an eighteenth-century original. The forged-looking welds are done electrically, but surface treated after welding to look like hand forging.

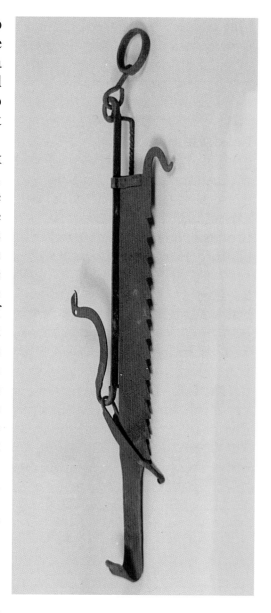

**Overall Length:**
**51 1/2"(minimum)**
**69" (maximum)**

Construction: Steel plate, rod and bar are the materials that make up the structure of this device. Steel plate has been used for the wide, flat saw tooth hook. The top of the hook has a dog leg lifting handle, welded in place. A retainer loop has been riveted to the top of the saw tooth hook.

The hanger bar is assembled from many small pieces cut to size from steel bar and strapping. They are formed to shape and electrically welded together. The pawl that engages the saw teeth is formed from two pieces and electrically welded at the point that joins the lift arm.

Cold chisel decorations are hammered into all the flat surfaces of the trammel and on the edges of the saw teeth. Some wear is ground into the edges of the large hanging hook at the bottom of the trammel.

Finish: The surface of this device is treated with a corrosive process that recreates the rust and pitting of centuries. A final wax coating is applied to stabilize the rust and give it the luster of a restored antique.

**Fake Tip-offs**

**1.** The entire construction of the trammel should be looked at from the standpoint of what parts would be expected to show signs of actual use-induced wear. Parts that loop around each other should have worn surfaces on every part where they touch. The inside of the pawl should be worn from its contact with the ratchet teeth. The teeth should also show an appropriate amount of wear. There are no such signs of wear on this fake.

**2.** The steel strapping of the lift handle on this fake is made from the same size stock as the hanger bar. On the original antique, the pieces would have been different sizes due to its hand-forged construction.

*Part of the lift handle, pawl and saw tooth hook are seen in this close-up.*

# Double Trammel 129

In France, they are called crémaillères. They are, in fact, double trammels that were used before the advent of iron cranes. They were suspended from a fixed point in very large fireplaces by the large iron ring at the top.

The fireplaces where these devices were used were large enough for a man to stand in upright. The decorative iron work was completely visible to people outside the fireplace. Today, however, most of our fireplaces are much smaller and these trammels are relegated to a decorative role. Our piece has been copied from a seventeenth-century original.

Construction: The inverted heart-shaped hanger is assembled primarily from steel bar that is cut to size, formed to shape and electrically welded together. At the heart point, the preformed steel bar is electrically welded together with decorative interior pieces, with the ring

**Overall Width: 21 1/4"**
**Overall Length:  56 1/2" (minimum)**
**72" (maximum)**

retaining loop formed after the welding operation. The heart sides slope down with a forged twist to the circular pads at the bottom. These pads are manufactured as separate details and are electrically welded on both sides to the heart frame. The bar frame then twists and curves up to a center pad that, when electrically welded, completes the outside of the heart frame. A square decorative piece is welded in place on this pad, top and bottom. The curling steel tendrils and the center flat diamond are then welded in place. The remaining details, hanger eyes, ring and decorative clips are added to complete the heart hanger.

The two hanging trammels are then fabricated in a very similar manner. The saw-toothed flat section is made from steel sheet that is cut to size, decorated with a coarse indented pattern, and electrically welded to what look like hand-forged details. The steel hanger bar and pawl arm are also cut from steel stock and electrically welded to obtain the form required. All the electric welds are finish ground and cosmetically hammered to create a hand-forged look.

Finish: The last operation in the manufacture of a fake antique is disguising the marks of its modern birth. To do this effectively and be able to fool most of the people most of the time, a corrosive process is used. The rust and surface pitting it produces are what you might expect to see on a real seventeenth-century device of this type.

Just lately, the forgers have been adding a new dimension of a restored look to their iron pieces. A wax finish is applied over the rust to stabilize the corrosive action and give the iron the luster of a restored antique.

## Fake Tip-offs

**1.** The entire construction of the trammel should be looked at from the standpoint of what parts would be expected to show signs of actual use-induced wear. Parts that loop around each other should have worn surfaces on every part where they touch. The inside of the pawl should be worn from its contact with the ratchet teeth. The teeth should also show an appropriate amount of wear. There are no such signs of wear on this fake.

2. Electric welding can be detected at the diamond point decoration of the inverted heart-shaped hanger. The iron curls show added material from the welding wire used in the assembly process. The square retainer at the top of the ratchet also shows the same effect.

# Trammels and Gridirons Summary

All of the trammels and gridirons described in this chapter are of European origin. American designs vary significantly from these.

There is no one foolproof method of determining a piece's authenticity. You have to study the manufacturing methods used both by hand forging and electric welding. There are very subtle little mistakes made by the fakers trying to duplicate a hand-forged look. By themselves they could easily be dismissed, but together they do give a clear picture of how and when a piece was made.

Grinding is one of the most common mistakes made. Hand forging does not add material to a weld joint, but electric welding does. The faker tries to remove as much of the added material as possible. Many times, too much of the added material is left. Sometimes too much is removed. Both conditions are signs of modern manufacture.

When you are not sure of a piece, take your time and examine it closely for the detail mistakes that could give away its true age.

# IX. Carved Wooden Figures

## Contents

# Bellhop Card Tray

Originally these novelty figures were used as card trays or as ashtray holders. They have been manufactured for years, in many different designs of both ethnic and occupational figures. This one has been made in the image of a bellhop with a serving tray.

Construction: The body of the bellhop is carved from a 2" thick board, with full detail on both sides. The two arms are carved out of boards and glued in place on each side of the body. The turned wood tray is assembled to the arms by gluing and doweling. The base is also turned from wood and assembled in the same fashion. The completed figure is then sanded, removing most of the minor blemishes and leaving the surface ready for primer.

Finish: The bellhop is primed and painted with various color paints. A little accelerated wear, a coat of wax and the resulting finish looks sixty years old.

## Fake Tip-off

This is a fake form of a twentieth-century collectible. The head profile is of a native Indonesian. An authentic piece was never made using that image.

**Overall Height: 38 ³/₄"**
**Overall Depth:  13"**

# Bellhop Card Tray　　　131

Sometimes called tip trays in the United States, these figures were also used to hold calling cards and ashtrays. Many were just flat profiles cut from boards with painted details. On this one, however, the details are all carved into the wood. The belt line of his trousers, his ears, nose, hat, shoes and even the drape of his sleeve have been carved.

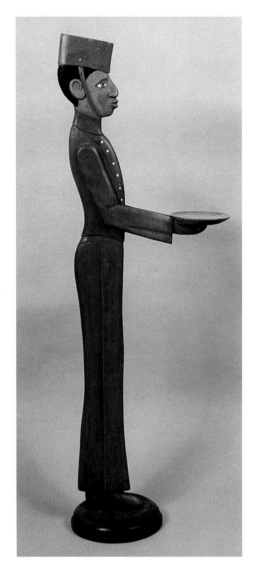

**Construction:** The body of the bellhop is cut from a 2" thick board. All the body details are fully carved on both sides. Two arms, cut out of boards, are glued and doweled in place, one on each side of the body. A turned tray is glued and doweled to the top of the hands. The base, also turned in wood, has been assembled in the same fashion. The completed figure is then finish sanded, removing most of the minor blemishes and leaving the surface ready for primer.

**Finish:** The bellhop is primed and gets a top coating of various color paints. Then it receives a little accelerated wear and a coat of wax. The result is a finish that looks sixty years old.

## Fake Tip-off

See data sheet #130 for a description.

**Overall Height: 39"**
**Overall Depth:  13 ³/₈"**

# Sitting Pig                                                132

Pig figures are great country collectibles. This naive version of a sitting pig has been carved out of wood, with a piece of curled iron rod for a tail. It has a semi-aged finish and, with very little extra conditioning, could really be believable as an antique carving.

Construction: The pig is carved out of solid wood in basically three components: the front legs, ears and body. They are precarved, then assembled together by gluing and doweling. The front leg joints are filleted with plastic body compound and smoothed into the body contour. A hole drilled in the back side of the pig serves as an anchor for the curled iron tail.

Finish: The painted finish on this figure is a good one. The first coat is a light red primer. The top finish coats have a cracking agent added to them, resulting in a nicely aged-looking condition. There has been some scuffing and wearing of the paint that has added a natural feeling to the artificially cracked paint.

**Fake Tip-off**

Check the smooth fillets of the front leg joints. If the finish scratches show the grey colour of plastic body filler, the figure is fake.

**Length:** 14 3/4"
**Width:** 5 1/4"
**Height:** 12 1/2"

# Carousel Pig 133

The original of this was a carousel figure that was either fixed to the deck of the turntable or was mounted on an oscillating shaft. It is a pretty good re-creation of a carousel pig. The paint finish has been aged and received some minor distressing, giving credibility as an original piece.

Construction: The trunk of the body serves as a mounting for all the detail parts. The tongue, tusks and ears have been carved separately and glued in place on the head. The head, which has been detail-carved by itself, has been glued and doweled to the body. The four legs and saddle back have been carved individually and then glued and doweled to the body. All of these glue joints have had fillets, made of grey plastic body filler. They have been sanded smoothly into the contours of the body. The saddle tassels have been carved and glued in place.

**Overall Length: 48 1/2"**
**Width: 10 3/4"**
**Overall Height: 23"**

Finish: The carved woodwork has been coated with a salmon-colored primer and then top coated with finish colors that crack upon drying. It has also received some manufactured wear and scuffing designed to fake an antique look.

## Fake Tip-off

**1.** Check the body contoured fillets for scratches. If the color of grey plastic body filler is evident, the pig is a fake.

**2.** The marks and wear of attachment to a carousel are missing. On an authentically old animal, there would be considerable evidence of this.

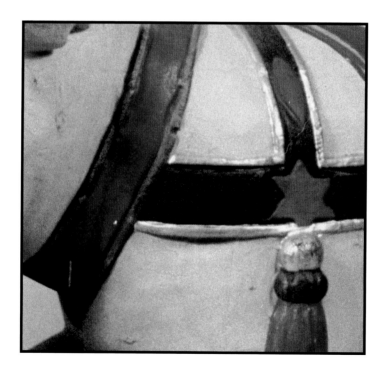

**Overall Length:  38"**　　　　**Width: 10"**　　　　**Overall Height: 51"**

# Carousel Horse 134

A soft, easy-to-work native wood was chosen for this animal because of the tremendous amount of detail to be carved. The horse is a full-size copy of a turn-of-the-century carousel figure. Its colorfully painted surface has been aged to reflect its reputed ninety years of life.

Construction: The head, all four legs, the saddle back and the ears are carved separately. They are glued and doweled to the main part of the wooden body. Where they meet the body, the joint lines are carved to a rough contour. Plastic body compound is then used to develop the smooth surface necessary for the final finish.

A hole drilled in the back end of the horse and real horse hair is glued in place, creating a very realistic-looking tail.

A black painted, crudely constructed iron mounting bracket has been provided. Inserted in a hole located in the horse's belly, the bracket provides temporary support, allowing the figure to stand in the prancing pose.

Finish: The horse is coated with salmon-tinted cracking primer and then top coated in finish colors. The paint is intentionally chipped and scuffed to create an antique look.

*A finish treatment of artificial age makes this horse look real.*

**Fake Tip-offs**

**1.** The wood used in this horse is too soft and light. Authentic carousel figures were carved from pine and similar woods.

**2.** Check the body contour fillets for scratches that reveal the grey color of plastic filler. Plastic filler is a modern development.

**3.** There is no evidence that this figure was ever used as part of a carousel.

**Overall Depth:** 16"
**Width Across Ears:** 16 ³/₄"
**Plaque Height:** 15 ¹/₂"
**Plaque Width:** 11 ¹/₄"

# Deer Head Trophy                    135

Many years ago, wooden trophy animal heads were made in quantity. There were many species of animals used as models, with the deer being one of the most common. Most of the old original heads were somewhat stylized and used paint colors that were definitely not natural. This deer head is very realistic looking, both in physical characteristics and coloration. It has been carved out of soft wood with glass eyes and real deer antlers to top it off.

Construction: The head has been carved from a block of soft wood. The ears have been carved separately, inserted in holes in the sides of the head and glued in place. The antlers have been assembled to the top of the head in much the same fashion. The plaque has been cut to size from hard wood and fastened to the deer's neck using glue and screws.
Plastic body filler has been used to develop the smooth contours of the deer's anatomy. It has also been used to cover the joint between the plaque and the deer's neck in a stylized bead.

Finish: The antlers have been left in their natural state. The rest of the head and plaque have been coated in salmon-colored primer and top coated with finish colors. There has been some minor wearing and scuffing of the finish, designed to create a feeling of age.

*The edges of both ears show some wood and finish deterioration.*

**Fake Tip-offs**

**1.** Grey plastic body filler used in contour fillets is a twentieth-century development. It can be seen in the finish scratches and fillet cracks.

**2.** Salmon-colored primer showing in the worn areas is an indication of modern manufacture.

# Lamb Bookend

The lamb and book are carved from soft native woods. The pieces are glued and doweled together to form a pretty, folksy-looking bookend. Despite being mass-produced in great quantities, the animal's detail is quiet good and can provide an excellent country decorating touch.

Construction: The lamb's wooden parts of front legs, head and body are carved to a rough shape separately. They are then glued and doweled together to form the rough animal shape. The lamb profile is finish carved and glued and doweled to the top of the precarved wooden book.

Finish: The entire assembly of lamb and book has been finished in a red primer with top coats of various colors. This piece has had no premature aging treatment. However the normal wear and tear of handling has caused some wearing of the painted surface. The exposure of the primer coat and base wood has given the piece some feeling of age.

**Fake Tip-off**

Red primer would not have been used on a real antique. Look for the red color of primer on the wooden edges and in finish scratches.

**Length: 11"    Width: 5"    Height: 9"**

# Carved Wooden Figures Summary

**T**he colorful carved figures described in this chapter have characteristics that lead one to believe that all of them have been made by the same group of people. The facial characteristics of the bellhop figures would indicate a Malaysian origin. Their choice of raw materials and the fact that most of the wood chosen for carving has been a soft, easy-to-work type, similar to balsa, also reinforces that thinking. If I were to take a guess at the location, the island of Java would be my first choice.

There are several other indicators that identify "Fabulous Fakes". Almost all of the carved wooden figures have a salmon-colored primer undercoat. You can generally see the pink edges of it when the paint surface chips. Also, when the manufacturer creates fake wear, the top finish coat of paint is selectively removed down to the pink primer. Not realizing it, he has provided a means of identifying the pieces' origin.

The fillets and smooth contours of these figures have not been attained by carving alone. Grey plastic body filler or compound has been extensively used to cut costs and reduce the amount of carving necessary to make an acceptable figure. A small scratch in a fillet should quickly reveal the grey color of the plastic compound.

In the United States, the climate is a lot drier than the figures' equatorial birthplace. The figures tend to lose a lot of moisture after being in this country for a while. The paint cracks, the glue joints open, seams open and the wood itself twists and splits open. When this happens you see everything, the salmon-colored primer, the balsa wood and the grey plastic filler.

# X. Wood, Iron & Brass Kitchenware

## Contents

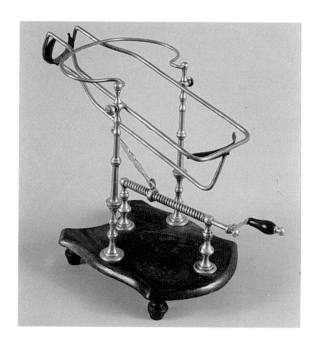

**Diameter: 27"**
**Board Thickness:** $^1/_2$"

# Painted German Breadboard 137

Old breadboards, taken from the kitchens of Europe, have been decorated in a manner that looks original. This particular breadboard was chosen as an example because of the variety of techniques used to create that impression. A very old nineteenth-century board, with an owner's name and original blue paint on the back side, provided the basic starting point for the faker. To that field of blue were added the fern-like fronds of white and the orange-yellow flowers created in a style reminiscent of Norwegian rosemaling.

Construction: The breadboards are generally made of at least three pieces of pine. A narrow center piece is used to form the handle and to serve as a bonding member for the two side pieces. Two thick straps, dovetailed across the grain of the three boards, are used to keep them from warping and to provide a wear pad for the back side. This breadboard is old and has all the wear characteristics that you would expect to find on an old board.

Finish: The blue paint is original, as is the wear on the dovetailed straps. A vestige of the name, Arthur Böttger, was found under the dirt in the middle of the blue field.

The painted decoration was applied in its various colors between the dovetailed straps. The Böttger name is highlighted using the same white color as the decoration. The original blue paint had, over the years, attained a cracked and alligatored surface. When a new decoration is painted on, it is applied lightly so that most of the new paint does not flow into the cracks and crevices of the old finish.

After the new paint is dry, it is rubbed down lightly with wire wool and given a coat of staining wax. The results of this procedure are spectacular, as you can plainly see by the photographs.

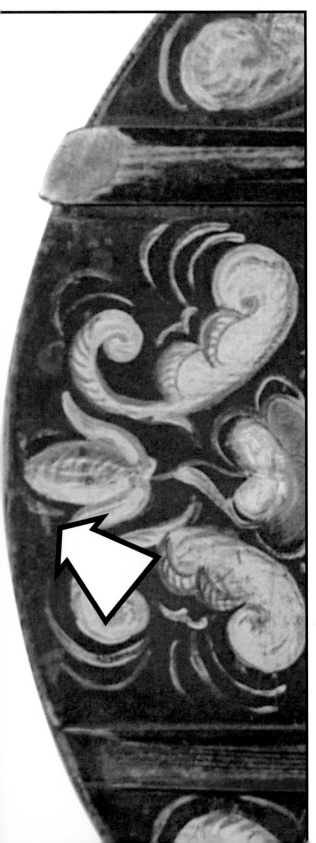

*Looking at the white tulip shape in the center of the right hand side of this close-up, you can see where white paint crosses over a bruise and scrape. It is an indication that the decoration was painted after the board had received a lot of wear.*

**Fake Tip-offs**

**1.** If the painted surface is cracked and the painted decoration flows across or into the crack, it can mean that there is a considerable age difference between the two. It means that the decoration is new.

**2.** With a magnifying glass, look at the decoration's painted surface. Because new paint takes a long time to cure and develop a hard surface, it scratches easily when first being worked with. The aging procedure for new paint requires it be rubbed with wire wool to wear the edges and high spots. This rubbing produces scratches on the new paint that would not appear on the old.

# Brass Trivet **138**

Trivets were used to hold teakettles near the hot coals of a fire. A piece of this type with its thin brass top plate was probably used for light heating, leaving the more ambitious chores to the heavy iron devices. The trivet was placed over the edge of a coal grate, sitting safely out of the direct fire. A kettle could then be placed on the top brass surface of the trivet, allowing it to sit safely near the fire's heat.

The rust on this trivet is the manufacturer's way of hiding the marks of its modern heritage. The crumbly rusted surface can and should be wire brushed and polished. You will find that this has been done to the examples that have found their way into today's marketplace.

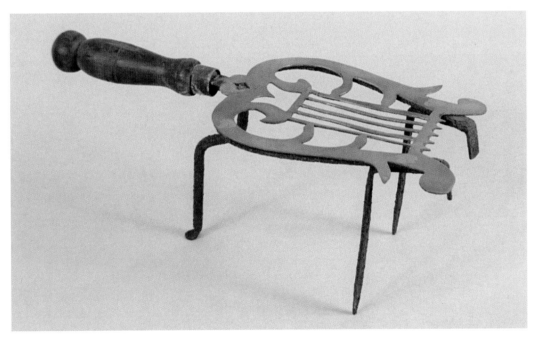

**Height: 5"**        **Width: 5 ¹/₂"**        **Length: 12 ¹/₄"**

Construction: A steel frame of 1/8" by 7/16" strapping is cut to size and formed into the shape required. The handle shank is sized from the same material and welded to the frame by electric welding. Two front legs, cut from a similar size strapping, are fabricated and riveted to the frame. The back leg is cut from 5/16" diameter round stock. One end is shouldered, inserted through a hole in the frame and riveted in place.

The brass top plate has been crudely cut from sheet stock and riveted in place on top of the frame with flush head rivets. The rivet heads have been brazed over to give a brass finish to their steel heads. A turned wooden handle with a brass collar is inserted over the shank of the steel frame.

Finish: The trivet assembly has been left, at this stage, without any form of surface finish.

## Fake Tip-off

**1.**Trivets were used on abrasive hearth surfaces. For this reason, there should be wear on the bottoms of the trivet legs. This wear would be evidenced by a smooth, worn flat surface if it is an antique piece.

*Removing the heavy scaling rust and polishing the brass will give it the look of a restored antique.*

# Port Tilter

# 139

The seriousness with which Victorians took their wine is amply demonstrated by the contraption called a port tilter. An open bottle of wine was inserted in the slightly angled cradle of the tilter. Pressure from the spring clip at the lower end of the cradle frame kept it in position and prevented sliding during the pouring operation. Pouring was accomplished by rotating the handle in a clockwise motion, with a glass in position under the open mouth of the bottle.

Construction: Because of the relatively complex nature of this assembly and the great number of small intricate shapes, cast brass was chosen as the material for most of the support structure and screw mechanism. The bottle cradle is fabricated from 3/16" diameter brass rod, cut to size, formed and brazed together.

Two thin steel leaf springs are fabricated and rivet fastened, one at each end of the bottle cradle. They are pre-rusted for age simulation.

The brass posts have threaded steel studs that extend through the wooden base and steel nuts to fasten them to the base. The wooden base has four bun feet that are doweled and glued in place. An interesting piece of attempted deception is

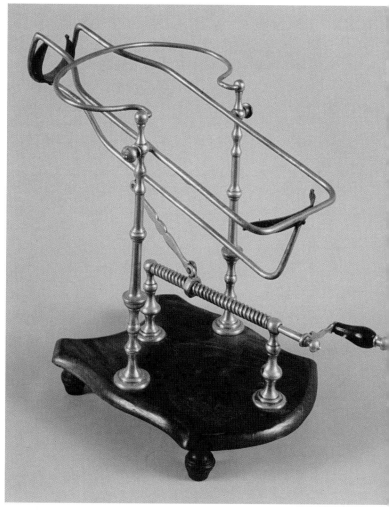

**Overall Height: 14"**
**(to the top of the lifting handle)**
**Base Width: 6 1/8"**
**Base Length: 8 1/4"**

the wood on the screw handle. It is drilled oversize to mimic a century of use.

Finish: All the brass on this piece has been polished to remove the braze flux and the residue of the casting process. After polishing, both the brass and the wood base have been given a coat of staining wax, designed to somewhat recreate the feeling of an aged accumulation of dirt.

**Fake Tip-offs**

**1.** There should be flat surfaces worn on the bottoms of the bun feet. It should be smooth wear with no indication of heavy scratches. The lacking of this is a good indication of a fake.

**2.** On the inside of the brass cradle there should also be wear evident from contact with bottles, if the tilter is truly old.

*The ring of staining wax can be seen on the posts and in the grooves of the long adjusting screw.*

# Iron Spoon 140

The spoon bowl has been made shallower than you would expect to see on an old spoon that was actually used in a kitchen. Outside of that one drawback, it does have an almost medieval appearance. A lightly chiseled decoration on the handle seems to provide a measure of increased gripping ability.

Construction: Sheet steel is cut to size and formed into the spoon bowl. The handle is cut and shaped from 1/8" by 7/16" steel strapping. The two pieces are electrically welded together. At the handle end a small piece of steel is welded and formed into the hanging loop.

All the welds have been finish ground to eliminate the marks of their electric welding. The handle has been marked with a cold chiseled decoration of a basic design that seems to be common in ancient iron implements.

Finish: The completed spoon has been treated to create a rusted surface that would pass for centuries of age.

## Fake Tip-off

**1.** Material size can be a good indicator of a pieces origin. Look at item #138. Notice that the steel strapping size is the same as the spoon's size. This would be highly unlikely on old pieces. Many of the fakes in this book share common material sizes. Prior to the machine age, there was no common material size.

**Overall Length: 19 ³/4"**
**Width: 3 ¹/16"**

# Iron Shovel                                        141

There are several details on this implement that give it a great deal of character. The handle twists and the rat tail loop at the end of the handle add eighteenth-century appeal to its construction.

Construction: The pan is cut from steel sheet and formed to shape. The pan sides are electrically welded at the two rear corners. The handle shank is cut from steel sheet and welded in a "V" cutout in the rear of the pan.
A piece of square steel bar is twisted in two places and electrically welded to the other end of the shank. A curl of formed steel is welded to the end of the handle to form a rat tail hanging loop. A small amount of cold chisel-formed decoration is done on the shank end of the handle.
All the electric welds are  finish ground to eliminate the marks of its modern manufacture.

Finish: The entire shovel is treated with a corrosive process, creating the rusted surface that one would expect to find on an eighteenth-century implement.

**Fake Tip-off**

Indications of electric welding can still be seen at the corners of the pan and several places on the twisted handle.

**Overall Length: 24 ³/₈"**                          **Width: 5 ¹/₂"**

# Iron Toasting Fork 142

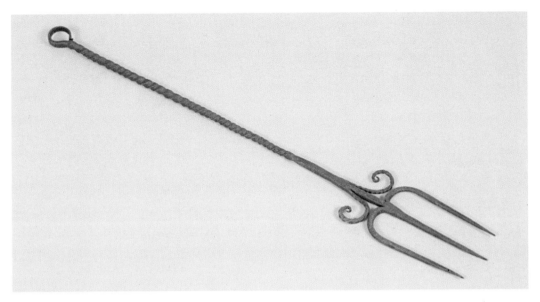

**Overall Length: 21 ³/₁₆"**                    **Width: 3"**

The long handle of this fork safely allowed it to be used over an open fire for toasting or cooking food. In the seventeenth century, when the design of this fork is thought to have originated, craftsmen made every effort to combine function with a feeling of beauty. This modern copy has captured that feeling.

Construction: The long handle, cut from square steel bar, is gracefully twisted its entire length. One end is ground to a fine taper, forming the center tine of the fork. The outside tines are cut from steel rod, ground to form and electrically welded to the center tine. Two twisted steel curls are welded in place to the shank end of the handle.
At the other end of the handle a forged steel curl is welded, forming the hanging loop. All the welds are finish ground to eliminate the marks of modern manufacture.

Finish: A corrosive treatment has been used to rust the surface of the fork in a way that looks like a real antique.

**Fake Tip-off**

Examine the welded parts of the fork. You can see where electric welding material has been removed by finish grinding.

# Brass Skimmer 143

In the colonial kitchen, skimmers were used for a variety of tasks. Separating fats from liquids was its main job. The one that most of us can associate it with, however, is removing the heavy cream from the top of milk in wide, open settling pans. Utensils made of sheet brass are among the easiest to reproduce and fake. On this one, for example, the only part that could show some age, has been treated in the same manner as old pieces. On truly old pieces they quite frequently are polished to a high shine, effectively removing all the gentle traces of wear and age. To mimic the old pieces, the fakes are also polished to a high shine.

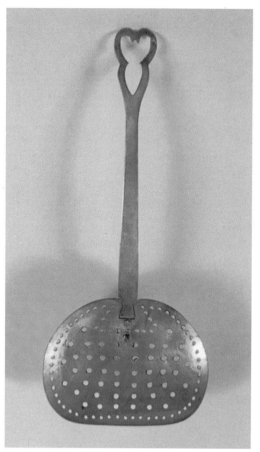

**Overall Length: 18"**
**Pan Width: 8"**

Construction: Thin brass sheet material is cut to size, drilled in a templated hole pattern with two different size holes, and formed into a shallow pan shape.
The handle is cut from 1/16" thick sheet into the proper shape and riveted to the skimmer pan using two copper rivets.
All the sharp edges on the sheet metal are deburred, including the holes. The holes are lightly countersunk on both sides to remove their burrs.

Finish: The entire skimmer is highly polished, effectively removing most of the tooling marks and leaving a finish that is quite common on a really old piece.

## Fake Tip-off

The countersinking of the pan holes has left a sharp shoulder on the edge of the hole. This is not a condition that you would expect to find on an old piece. Years of cleaning and scrubbing would have worn away any shoulder on a real antique.

# Star Pattern Skimmer 144

The irregular and somewhat crudely developed hole pattern of the pan has been done purposely to create the illusion of an ancient craftsman-produced piece. The perception that modern manufacturing techniques would not have produced this quality pattern is what the fakers are banking on to gain acceptance of their work as genuine antiques.

Construction: A piece of steel strapping 1/8" thick by 13/16" wide is cut to size. The center section is forged into a round configuration.
The loop end of the handle has two iron tendrils electrically welded to its butt end. After the welding cleanup, the tendrils are heated and bent into graceful loops. The brass pan is cut out of thin sheet material and drilled in a star pattern. A template is probably used to expedite the operation. After the drilling the pan is formed and its outer edge rolled over a wire to form a smooth rim. The pan is riveted to the handle with three copper rivets.

Finish: The handle is rusted to cover the electric welding and finish grinding marks. The brass pan and copper rivets are highly polished.

## Fake Tip-off

Rather than deburring the drilled holes by conventional methods, the faker has opted to crush the hole burrs. This has left the back side of the pan with a very rough surface. On a real antique, that surface would be worn smooth.

**Overall Length: 26"**
**Pan Diameter: 9"**

# Flower Pattern Skimmer

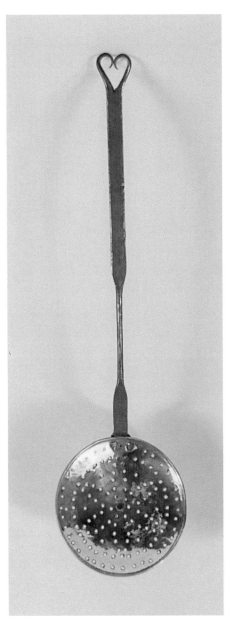

**Overall Length: 23 1/2"**
**Pan Diameter: 6 1/2"**

One distinctive feature of this utensil is the narrow waist of the handle. The metal is actually crimped and hammered into a nearly round configuration in this area. It looks as if it had been worked fairly cold and not forged at the fire. There certainly is no indication of high heat being involved in this operation.

The heart shaped hanging loop at the end of the handle does give the impression of being hand forged. However, this impression of hand forging has been created by modern technology and its electric welding.

Construction: Steel strapping, 1/8" thick by 11/16" wide, is cut to size. The waist is formed at the top end of the handle. Two tapered pieces of steel rod are electrically welded in place to form the heart shape. The weld area is then finish ground to remove excess weld material and contour it to the main part of the handle. The brass pan is cut from thin brass sheet and drilled to create the flower hole pattern that you see in the illustration. The pan is then formed and its edges rolled over a fine wire to form a smooth rim. The final operation is to rivet the pan to the handle with three copper rivets.

Finish: The handle on this example is lightly rusted. However, it is likely that some pieces will come through with the iron heavily corroded. The brass pan, in contrast, has been highly polished to remove the manufacturing marks and add a semblance of wear.

## Fake Tip-offs

**1.** The hole burrs on the back of the pan have not been removed. They have been crushed flat leaving a very rough surface. On an authentically old piece, this surface would be worn smooth.

**2.** The use of electric welding can be seen at the point of the heart on the handle end. A small blob of melted metal has been left on the inside of the point.

*You can see the excess metal left as a result of electric welding.*

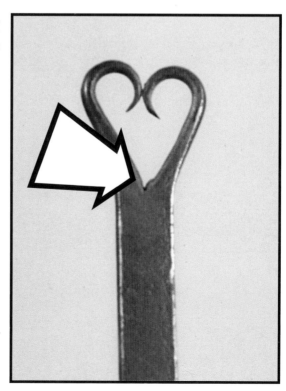

# Wood, Iron & Brass Kitchenware Summary

The breadboard, item #137, is basically an old board that someone has enhanced with some new paint. The fact that the piece is old to begin with sets the stage for believing that the faked decoration is old as well.

All the metal utensils described in this chapter have a common pattern of construction techniques. The steel pieces have utilized the low heat of electric wire feed welding and finish grinding in their manufacture. The brass pieces have not had their holes deburred in the normal way; instead they are crushed flat against the pan sheet. There is a commonality of material size that is a clear indication of their being made by the same factory. These common details preclude the possibility of their being genuine antiques.

# XI. Metal Toys

## Contents

**Overall Height: 10 ³/₄"**      **Base Width: 4 ⁵/₈"**      **Base Length: 9 ³/₄"**

# Mickey Mouse Pull Toy            **146**

The toy is designed to roll on three wheels and be pulled by a string through the hole on the front edge of the chassis. The legs of the mouse are rigidly fixed to the chassis platform. The upper torso and arms pivot and allow the mouse to move up and down as the crank turns with the front wheel.

Construction: Thin steel sheet is used for all the details of this toy. An interesting note is that the material thickness is much heavier than you would expect to find on an action toy of this type. A commercially manufactured toy would have been design-engineered to allow much thinner material and a lithographed surface finish. The chassis on this piece is hand cut out of thin steel sheet, heavy enough to maintain its shape. Bent over tabs provide a bearing surface for the two wheel axles. The thin steel wheels are 2 1/4" in diameter.

Two thin legs are fastened to the chassis with bent over tabs. The torso of the mouse pivots between the two fixed legs. Two pivoting arms and crank are fastened to the front wheel.

Finish: The entire toy has been hand painted. The steel material does not show any sign of a primer being used.

**Fake Tip-offs**

**1.** Manufacturers of toys using the likeness of Mickey Mouse are required by law to be licensed by the Disney people. The licensing information should be found somewhere on every legally authorized toy. You will find that this version of Mickey Mouse has not been licensed and the faker has not attempted to mark the toy in any way.

**2.** True production toys are generally made of very thin lithographed sheet steel. Excellent color and detail are attained by using this material. This toy, on the other hand, is made of very heavy sheet steel and is hand painted. These two characteristics peg this toy as a fake.

# Dancing Lady Teeter Toy     **147**

The dancing lady uses a counterweight hanging below the balance point to provide the stability for the toy. The gowned lady attached above the balance point supplies the entertainment value. When you push a little on the counterweight, the lady rocks back and forth in a dancing motion. The tall stand allows the counterweight to swing freely.

**Construction:** The lady figure and the right angle piece between her feet are cut from one piece of .032" thick sheet steel. A small "V" of sheet steel is soldered to the bottom of the right angle piece to provide lateral stability. A long curved sheet steel arm, with a heavy counterweight attached, is riveted to the end of the right angle piece at the figure's feet.

The stand is made with a dished saddle for the balance point. Two long rods, riveted to the saddle, extend down to the round base. Here they are also riveted in place.

**Finish:** The dancing lady has been mildly corroded to simulate age. Finish colors have been hand painted in a 1920's style. The figure has both sides painted as though it was three dimensional.

### Fake Tip-off

An original toy of this type would show some sign of wear on the pivot and saddle. This fake has no evidence of wear. The pivot points are sharp and the saddle has a smooth painted surface.

**Overall Height: 21 ³/₄"**
**Base Diameter: 4 ¹/₄"**

# Little Red Riding Hood Teeter Toy   148

The little girl in the American version of Little Red Riding Hood wears a red cape with a hood. This girl has on what looks to be a red riding helmet. That and the bottle of wine protruding from her picnic basket indicate a European design. While interesting because of the number of characters, it certainly is crudely made and lacks the ingenuity of other toys illustrated in this chapter.

Construction: The moving part of this toy is cut out of one piece of .032" thick sheet steel. The balance piece is part of that cutout and is twisted ninety degrees to provide lateral stability for the rocking movement. The circular counterweight is crimped on the curved arm that extends down under the balance platform.

The base of the toy consists of four pieces. The saddle or balance platform is riveted to a formed sheet steel base, using two long shouldered rods.

Finish: The metal is primed and painted in bright primary colors. The item in her right hand is highlighted in red. This is a painting technique used in many native cultures to emphasize an important feature.

**Fake Tip-off**

An original toy of this type should show some signs of wear on the pivot and saddle. This fake has no evidence of wear.

**Overall Height: 13 3/4"**
**Base Size: 4" x 6 1/4"**

# Cowboy Teeter Toy 149

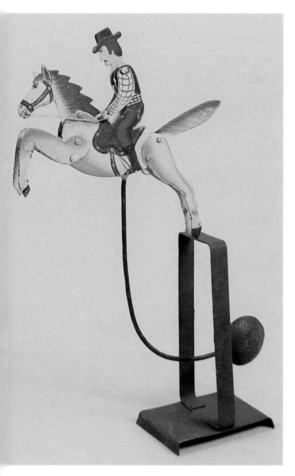

**Overall Height: 18"**
**Base Size: 4" x 5 ³/₈"**

The figure sizing has been accurately done with a slightly folksy touch. The horse is cantilevered off the balance saddle, giving the impression that it is about to fall off. That, combined with the movement of the man's head and arms and the horse's head and tail, will create some lively action.

Construction: Sheet steel 1/16" thick is used for all the flat details of this teeter toy. The body of the horse is riveted together in a fixed position with the four legs. The main counterweight is attached to the belly of the horse with a thin curved steel rod. The horse's head and tail are counterweighted to provide movement. The cowboy's arms move through their attachment to the horse's head with the reins. His head moves are made possible by an attached counterweight. The two back legs of the horse are riveted together to strengthen them.

The base is fabricated from sheet steel and riveted together to form a very stable platform for the movement of the toy.

Finish: All the parts of this toy are lightly primed and painted in finish colors that are appropriate for the figures. There has been no intentional rusting on this toy.

## Fake Tip-off

Because of its complexity and the many moving parts of the horse and rider, all the joints of a truly old toy should exhibit signs of wear. This would be evidenced by scratches and looseness at the point of movement. Also the pivot and saddle should have signs of wear. This fake shows none of this wear.

# Black Dancer Puppet

**150**

The trick to handling this toy is proper manipulation of its movements at the end of a string. With a little practice, you can get the puppet to tap dance and perform in an entertaining fashion. Both the dancer's legs are jointed at the hips and knees. His arms are jointed at the shoulder

The black clog-shaped shoe indicates a Dutch influence and European origin. The toy gives the feeling of late nineteenth-century production. However the contemporary tie and jacket give away its true age.

Construction: The puppet is cut out of 1/32" thick sheet steel. Two pieces are riveted together with spacers to form the double thick body. The arms are offset riveted to each shoulder. Their downward travel is restrained by the body spacer rivets. The two legs are riveted in place with no restriction on their travel. The lower portion of the legs are riveted on opposite sides of the knees to keep the puppet action in balance. The riveted joints are all free to move with the jiggling action of the puppet. At the top point of the puppet's hat, a few links of wire chain are attached to help magnify the action of the toy.

Finish: Slightly rusted prior to finishing, the figure is coated with a red primer and then finish painted.

**Fake Tip-offs**

**1.** The form of the toy is your first indication that it might be fake. It is highly unlikely that you would be able to find a real antique toy of this type.

**2.** Look for the joint wear of an old toy. This fake has no wear at all.

**Overall Height: 11 1/2"**
**Overall Width: 8 1/2"**
**(maximum)**

# Parrot Teeter Toy                    151

There are no moving parts other than the parrot itself. It is a pretty basic silhouette type of toy. The heavy counterweight attached to the lower end of its tail provides the pendulum action necessary to keep the parrot moving after initially being rocked.

The stand has a curved saddle plate that keeps the parrot pivot from walking off.

Construction: The parrot, in spite of its three dimensional appearance in the illustration, is cut from 1/16" thick steel sheet. A small "V" piece of steel is fastened to the bird's foot to serve as the pivot for its rocking action. A lead base alloy is used in the casting of the toy's counterweight. The weight's surface has a peened finish that provides a better base for the final finish and an interesting texture to the metal.

The platform base is fabricated from sheet steel and riveted together. The resulting assembly is very stable and rugged.

Finish: All the metal pieces of this toy have been primed and finish painted in the bright colors of the original bird.

**Fake Tip-off**

A toy of this type would show some indication of wear on the pivot and saddle. The pivot points shown here are sharp with no evidence of wear and the saddle plate has a smooth painted surface.

**Overall Height: 17 1/2"**
**Base Size: 4" x 5 3/8"**

# Bearded Dwarf Teeter Toy     152

Europe was probably responsible for the origin of this toy. The dwarf-like figure is reminiscent of a fairy tale-type character. The waistcoat, breeches and conical hat are in line with that thinking.
There has been a full-blown effort to artificially age this toy. Rusted metal, chipped paint and a thin watery stain have combined to create a visual appearance of reasonable age.

Construction: The dwarf figure and counterbalance arm are cut from one piece of 1/32" thick sheet steel. The pivot points under his legs are cut as part of the figure and twisted ninety degrees to provide a stabile rocking motion. A heavy counterweight is fastened to the end of the counterbalance arm.
The stand for this toy is cut and formed from steel sheet 1/32" thick.

Finish: The entire toy is coated with red primer and finished in the various colors.

**Fake Tip-off**

The pivot points and saddle surface on an old toy would show some signs of wear. This fake does not.

**Overall Height: 10"**
**Base Size: 3 1/2" x 4"**
**(across the legs)**

# Rolling Clown Toy 153

A slight push sends this clown into a tumbling roll down the parallel bars. The offset head and leg of the figure act as a balance for the body and allow it to roll smoothly, although it looks like it is tumbling. The finish on this toy has been distressed to give the appearance of age.

Construction: The clown figure is cut from 1/8" thick steel sheet. A headed rod is inserted through a hole and brazed in place with an additional stop on the far end. The pieces of the parallel bars are cut to size from steel rod and weld assembled together. Stops are brazed in place on the horizontal rod end. The rod assemblies are then welded to a preformed sheet steel base.

Finish: The steel is coated with a red primer and finished with various color paints, as shown in the illustration. The finished clown figure has been distressed with chipping paint and a scrubbed dirt finish.

**Fake Tip-off**

The rolling bars are electric welded to the vertical base.

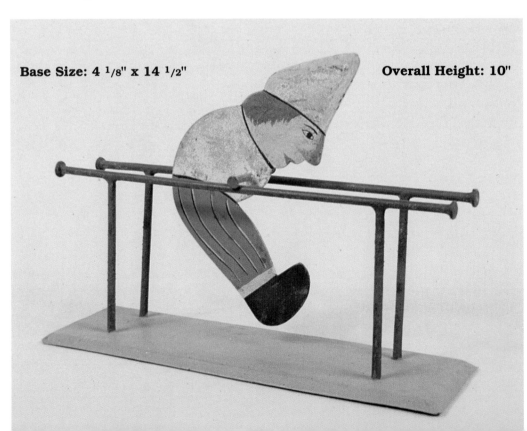

Base Size: 4 1/8" x 14 1/2"     Overall Height: 10"

# Metal Toys Summary

Most of the sheet metal toys that have been manufactured since the mid-nineteenth century have been mass produced in factories that employed the most modern manufacturing techniques available. Their products were engineered to get the most for the least amount of cost. Not only was the raw material cheaper, but the manufacturing of the toy was less expensive. Lighter molds, less energy to run machinery, lighter dies for cutting to size, ease in handling and reduced shipping costs all contributed to the increased profit margins for the manufacturer.

You should take notice of the common thread of material sizing for the sheet metal toys illustrated in this chapter. All the toys seem to be manufactured by the same group of people. The material sizes chosen are too heavy for normal production-type toys. The assembly methods used are time consuming and are not practical for mass production. In addition, all the metal pieces have been hand cut to size. This type of manufacturing engineering would not have been done on a collectible production toy.

# XII. Decorative Arts

## Contents

**Frame Overall Width: 21 $^3/_4$"**
**Frame Overall Length: 25 $^3/_4$"**

**Painting Width: 11 $^1/_2$"**
**Painting Length: 15 $^1/_2$"**

**Label Width: 2 $^7/_8$"**
**Label Length: 4 $^1/_8$"**

# English Dog Painting 154

Three English dogs are portrayed in a serene country setting with a farmhouse just visible through the trees. The detail of the painting is concentrated on the images of the dogs, tree trunks and the farmhouse. The rest of the painting has been done in an impressionistic style.

Construction: The painting is done on canvas and artificially aged. The wood frame is a very good copy of a late Victorian gold frame. A fake label is printed on an old-looking buff-colored paper and glued to the top edge of the frame. The buff-colored finish of the paper is printed on the surface of the label. The base paper is similar to white bond. The label is printed as follows:

## BIGGS & SONS
### CARVERS, GILDERS
AND
### PICTURE RESTORERS

*3 L CONDUTT ST BOND STREET*
## LONDON

**LOOKING GLASSES SUPPLIED, OLD FRAMES REGILT**

Finish: The front surface of the frame has received a liberal dusting of dirt that has accumulated in the crevices of the heavy ornamentation. The back surface of the painting and frame has been rubbed with a light abrasive. The resulting finish looks worn and old. Even the fake label that is applied to the back is half worn off.

An interesting thing about this fake painting is its overall condition. No one has tried to damage either the frame or the painting to give a greater dimension to the illusion of age. They are both in great shape except for the wear on the back.

**Fake Tip-offs**

**1.** The buff-colored label is supposed to simulate faded paper. It becomes quite apparent that the label has the faded look printed on it when you remember that fading goes through the entire piece of paper, not just on the surface. In the close-up of the label, where it has been worn, you can easily see the bleached white of the new paper.

**2.** If the picture was as old as the faker would like you to think it is, there certainly would be minor damage or wear to the frame. Over a period of time, wood shrinks and plaster dries out. The combination of these two things does cause some breakage in the frame decoration. On this frame there is none of that evidence.

*The label clearly shows the new paper under the printed surface.*

*The difference in the painting detail can be seen between the dogs and the background.*

# English Rooster Painting          155

Most of the elements of an old painting are present in this fake rendering of an English barnyard scene. The mood has been set by the old stonework and the thatched roof cottage in the background. Typical barnyard residents, involved in their everyday life and death struggles, round out the painting.

Construction: The painting is done on canvas and artificially aged. The frame is burl veneered with an inner moulding around the painting and an outer edging in a similar black color.

**Frame Overall Width: 13 1/4"**
**Frame Overall Length: 15 1/4"**

**Label Width: 3"**                    **Painting Width: 7 1/2"**
**Label Length: 4 1/8"**              **Painting Length: 9 1/2"**

Finish: The veneer is washed with a black staining compound that accumulates in the cracks and crevices of the veneer. The result is a stunning finish that really looks old.

The back of the painting has a fake label applied in a manner similar to the one on the back of the English Dog Painting # 154. The label and the entire edge of the frame are rubbed with a light abrasive, creating a worn-looking surface. In contrast the front and outer edge of the frame have not been damaged or worn at all. The wood edges of the frame and its four corners are sharp and square.

## Fake Tip-offs

**1.** Again, as on the dog painting, the label has been worn through to the new white paper. Its faded condition was only printed on the surface. The printed information is exactly the same as the label of the dog painting.

**2.** On an authentically old frame, the mitred corners would not be square and true. Wood dries and shrinks at different rates, resulting in uneven corner joints. Also, there would be some deterioration of the sharp edges and corners of the frame.

*The signature of the supposed artist, Hunt, as it appears in the lower right hand corner of the painting.*

# Chinese Ginger Jar

# 156

Earthenware has been used for centuries as a material for ginger jars. This re-creation, with its rotund shape and domed, loose fitting cover, has been decorated with a blue washed figural design. The fish and flowers are traditional Chinese in character, though somewhat cruder than you would expect to see on a truly old piece of this quality.

**Overall Height: 8"**
**Jar Diameter: 7 1/2"**
**Base Diameter; 4 1/4"**

Construction: The pottery jar bottom is slip cast in a divided mold. It is allowed to harden in the mold. When removed from it, the separation line that has been left by the mold is smoothed away prior to its biscuit or initial firing. The biscuit firing is done at a temperature of about 1000 degrees centigrade.

Finish: After cooling, a coating of wax is applied to the jar rim and the base ring. This wax keeps the glaze coating from adhering to it and allows a glaze-free surface for resting during the final firing.

The jar is hand-painted with blue figures and patterns, then dipped in a tin glaze. The jar cover has been formed using the same procedure outlined for the bottom piece. Both pieces then receive their final firing, at temperatures approaching 1000 degrees centigrade. With temperatures this high, the borax in the glaze tends to boil and form bubbles. Some of these bubbles still remain after the pieces are cooled. After the firing and while the pottery is still hot, the pieces are removed from the kiln and placed in a nest of wet straw and grasses. Some of the wet straw is thrown into the interior of the jars. The straw material ignites and the carbon produced by the straw burning colors the unglazed surfaces and penetrates into the glaze cracks.

It should be noted that the glaze often crazes due to the sudden change in temperature brought about by exposure to the wet straw. The darkened edges and crazed glaze cracks produced give the ginger jar a wonderful aged look. This burning procedure is a technique similar to the Japanese glaze firing process called Raku.

*The dark staining, shown here on the bottom of the jar, is a result of cooling in the wet straw.*

### Fake Tip-offs

**1.** On old pieces you will find light surface scratching brought about by normal use.

**2.** The faker has flooded the market with this form. If you have one, view it with suspicion. It probably is fake.

# Chinese Baluster Jar                    157

**Overall Height: 16 ¹/₄"**
**Jar Diameter: 8 ¹/₈"**
**Base Diameter; 6 ³/₄"**

The baluster jar, so named for its shape, was a piece designed for storage as well as decoration. The blue flowers and patterns have been applied with more attention paid to their detail than the ginger jar #156.

Construction: The baluster-shaped jar has been hand thrown on a potter's wheel, in contrast to the ginger jar, which was slip cast. The bottom of this piece is heavier and blended in a smooth radius on the inside where the sides meet the bottom. This jar, like the last, was biscuit fired prior to the application of the glaze coat. The firing temperature is close to 1000 degrees centigrade.

Finish: After the jar cools to near room temperature, a wax coating is applied to the rim of the top opening and the rim of the bottom surface. Wax is also applied to the mating surface of the jar top. This wax coating keeps the glaze from adhering to it and allows a glaze-free surface to form for resting during the final firing.

The baluster jar and its cover are hand-painted with a blue decoration and dipped in a tin glaze. Both pieces then receive their final firing at temperatures approaching 1000 degrees centigrade. The borax in the glaze tends to boil at the high firing temperature and forms bubbles in the finish. Many of these remain after the piece is cooled.

When the jar is removed from the kiln after the final firing, a procedure similar to Japanese Raku is used. After the firing and while the pottery is still hot, the pieces are removed from the kiln and placed in a bed of wet straw and grasses. Some of the wet straw is thrown into the interior of the jar. The straw material ignites. The carbon produced by its burning colors the unglazed surfaces and penetrates into the glaze cracks. It should be noted that the glaze often cracks and crazes due to the sudden change in temperature brought about by the exposure to the wet straw.

*The burned rim and stained glaze cracks are the result of the Raku burning.*

## Fake Tip-offs

**1.** Light surface scratching, brought about by normal use, will be found on old pottery.

**2.** Because of the large quantity of fake pottery, a similar form should be viewed with suspicion.

# French Flower Basket                158

Woven wire has long been a favorite of garden lovers everywhere. Garden furniture, planters, plant stands and baskets abound in a variety of designs. This oval French flower basket has been re-created from one of those designs. Its woven wire, delicately interlaced, has been formed into a very high quality, weather resistant, decorative container.

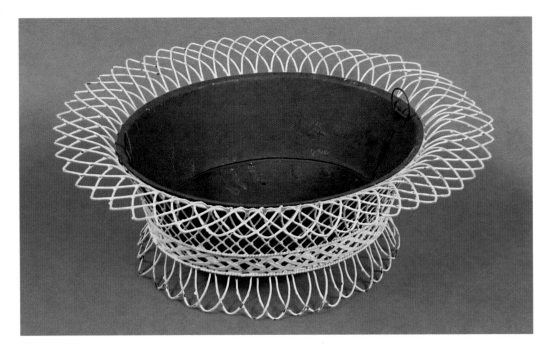

**Basket**
**Overall Length: 18 3/4"**
**Overall Width: 16 3/8"**
**Overall Height: 6 3/4"**

**Tin Liner**
**Length: 13 1/4"**
**Width: 10 3/4"**
**Height: 4 3/4"**

Construction: A small, oval, heavy wire ring is formed from .125" diameter soft steel wire or rod. It is electrically welded into a 8" by 10 1/2" closed ring. To this ring are crimped fifty six .062" diameter wires in a criss-crossing pattern. A larger oval ring, 10 5/8" by 13 3/8", made from electrically welded .125" diameter steel wire or rod, is positioned inside the woven wire framework to serve as the top frame. It is fastened with a double wrap of tie wire to each cross point in the wire side.

Thirty-seven small lengths of .062" diameter wire are looped in a criss-crossing pattern and crimped to the same ring as the side wires. These serve as the base for the basket. In addition, there are six radial wires, wire wrapped at the center, that form the bottom support for the tin insert. Around the outside of the bottom oval ring, a woven quadruple wire braid with a double twisted wire edging is fastened in place with wire wraps.

The steel insert pan is made from three pieces of sheet tin, .028" thick. They are cut to size, formed to shape and fastened together with crimped seams. The pan rim is rolled and formed in a double thick flattened edge. A ring  handle is riveted in place, at the top edge of each end of the pan.

Finish: The pan is primed in an olive drab primer. The wire basket has been coated with a brown primer and finished in a flat white enamel.

## Fake Tip-off

Because of the exposure to moisture, it would be normal to see a fair amount of heavily rusted wire on an antique. This fake has none.

# Double Twist Flower Basket          159

The distinctive feature of this wire flower basket is the double twisted wire that has been used in most of its construction. It has given an almost textured feeling to an otherwise plain piece of wire. The small shape of the pan insert lends itself to an enclosure for potted plants rather than the planter type, shown in Item # 158.

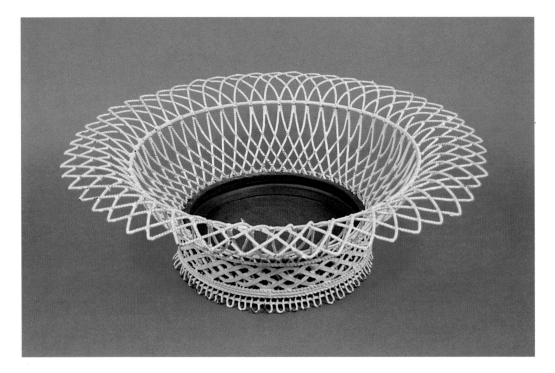

**Basket Diameter: 16"**
**Pan Insert Diameter: 7 3/8"**
**(maximum rim)**

**Basket Height: 5 3/4"**
**Pan Insert Height: 1"**

Construction: A base ring of heavy soft steel wire or rod, .125" diameter thick, is electrically welded into a ring, 7 1/2" in diameter. Fifty-two pieces of double twisted wire are formed to shape and are crimped to the ring to form the criss-cross pattern of the side wall. An intermediate ring, the same size and material as the base ring, is tied into place near the top of the basket. The double twisted wires are tied in two additional places, one near the rim of the basket and one halfway up the side wall.

Radiating out from the base ring are six wire lengths, tied at the center. There is a spiraling wire starting at the center and circling around, ending at the base ring. This wire is tied in place with wire wraps.

On the bottom of the base ring, a looping wire formed into a base is added, along with an additional support ring. These are tied in place with wire ties. Just above this ring, on the outside of the basket, a woven quadruple wire braid with a double twisted wire edging is fastened in place with wire wraps.

The insert pan is crudely formed from .030" thick sheet steel. It is a seamed and crimped construction with flattened double lip.

Finish: The pan insert is coated with an olive drab primer. The wire basket is primed in a dark brown and finished in a flat white enamel.

## Fake Tip-off

Watering flowers quickly brings on rust. No amount of paint can completely stop it. On a truly old basket you could expect to see a fair amount of heavily rusted wire. This fake has none.

# Hanging Flower Basket 160

The Victorian spirit is embodied in this frilly wire flower basket. Wire has been used throughout the entire construction of this piece. Even the hanging chain is wire. The only thing not wire is the pan insert. This basket can take both potted and directly planted flowers.

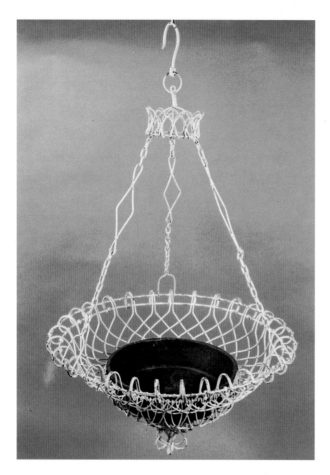

**Basket Diameter: 22 $^1/_4$"**
**Basket Height: 36 $^3/_4$"**
**(to top of hook)**
**Pan Insert Diameter: 12"**
**Pan Insert Height: 4"**

Construction: The main structural member is a heavy ring of welded wire that serves as the common member for the side wires' crimping. Sixty pieces of interlaced wire are formed and crimped to this ring. Two additional rings are formed, welded and wired in place at the top of the basket. The heavier ring serves as the crimping ring for the side wires.

The lighter top ring has three wire chains crimped to it in three places, equally spaced. The top ends of the chain are crimped to an interlaced wire, crown-shaped, hanger frame. A heavy hanger hook is securely wired to this frame.

The bottom section of the basket is formed from interlaced wire and securely fastened in place.

The tin pan insert, formed from .030" thick sheet steel, is a seamed and crimped construction with a flattened double lip. The lip serves as the support surface when inserted in the wire basket.

Finish: The pan insert is coated with an olive drab primer. The wire basket is primed in a dark brown and finished in a flat white enamel.

## Fake Tip-off

Water has an immediate effect on a woven wire planter. Truly old originals will display rusting brought on by water. This fake has no rust.

# Rose Handled Flower Basket 161

**Overall Height: 21 1/2"**
**Overall Length: 20 1/2"**
**Overall Width: 17"**
**Base Diameter: 5 7/8"**

The roses and their curling tendrils have been worked into the design of this basket in a way that makes them almost real. The embossed leaves and the red rose petals have been frozen in sculptured steel. A deep, watertight liner provides ample capacity for many cut flowers.

Construction: Three rings are formed from steel rod. They are welded together to form the basket base. From this base, welded steel rods rise to form the basket side. They are welded to a top ring of steel rod. A steel rod handle, wire wound at the center, is welded to the top ring of the basket.

The rose vine is preformed and finish ground to simulate curling vine tendrils. It is then electric welded in place. The stems are steel wire, cut to size and welded in place. The rose leaves are die-cut and formed. They are then welded in place. The roses themselves are die-cut in a flat condition. There are five different sizes of petals. They are formed, assembled together and welded in place.

The liner is fabricated from embossed steel in a formed and crimped seam configuration.

Finish: The liner and the basket frame have been finished in a golden brown color and the rose vine finished in green and red.

**Fake Tip-off**

The bottom of the basket shows no wear. A truly old one would have a flat surface worn on the three rings.

# Victorian Gilt Doll's Chair          162

Several years ago, at a small antiques auction in the midlands of England, I chanced upon what I thought was a Victorian doll's chair. I examined it as closely as I could with the curious crowd of auction-goers pressing in on all sides. It looked good. So when its time came to be sold, I joined in the spirited bidding for its purchase. When the auctioneer's hammer finally fell, I was the new owner of the chair. My investment was 150 Pounds Sterling, which converted to 300 dollars at the then current rate of exchange.

The chair I purchased at that auction is the fake we are going to talk about in this section.

The chair, with its gold gilt and elegant black decoration, presents a superficial image of a Victorian construction. The plank seat has been painted with two goldfinch birds and flowering apple tree branches. The moulded style back seems to be copying the lines of papier-mâché furniture, with its flowing rounded curves and painted designs. On the legs and seat edge, there is an appropriate amount of wear and distress.

The underside of the seat and chair frame exhibit the familiar grunge and ancient looking glue blocks. Positioned in the center of the underside is a worn and stained label claiming the chair to be made by Biggs and Sons.

**Overall Height: 17** 3/4"
**Width of Seat: 9** 5/8"
**Depth of Seat: 8** 11/16"

Construction: The chair is constructed in a traditional way. The back is made of six pieces of wood in a mortise and tenoned frame. The seat is cut out of a sheet of 5/16" thick plywood. The seat frame again has a similar mortise and tenoned frame. Corner glue blocks have been form fitted and glued in place. The front legs are lathe turned and the center hole on the open end plugged with compound. There is some minimal carving on the back frame and the front legs. The quality of this carving is very poor.

Finish: The entire chair has been given a coat of gesso, a gypsum prepared with glue and used prior to painting. Over the gesso, flat black enamel has been applied. The decorative images are then applied in their various colors. A thin coat of varnish finishes the process.

### Fake Tip-offs

**1.** If you examine the edge of the seat closely, the layers of wood indicating twentieth-century plywood can be seen.

**2.** The Biggs and Sons label is the same one found on the fake paintings #154 and #155, a clear indication that the chair is a fake.

*Good grunge and a fake label help make this chair look like an authentic antique.*

# Domed Wire Birdcage 163

|        | Dia. | Ht. |
|--------|------|-----|
| Size "A": | 2" x | 4" |
| Size "B": | 7 $^7/_8$" x | 13" |
| Size "C": | 9" x | 15 $^3/_4$" |
| Size "D": | 11" x | 17" |

Rusty wire is woven into a wide range of birdcage sizes. Miniature cages for crickets through larger sizes capable of housing several birds are created with the same style construction.

Construction: Strands of heavy steel wire are bent into a "U" shaped form. These pieces are cut to the desired height and grouped together into two sections. They are tied together at the top, with one group crossing under the other. A round wire grid serves as the tie point for the side wires. The ends are crimped to the outer ring of the base grid in an equally spaced pattern. Steel wire is formed into rings and fastened in lace with fine wire that is woven around the rings and the side wires. The ring reinforcement is done down the entire side of the cage in a random fashion.

The door to the cage interior has been made in the same way. Wires are cut and formed, then wound with fine wire to bind the pieces together.

A heavy piece of steel rod is cut and formed into a hanging hook for the cage. The hook retainer is a steel washer that is welded to the bottom end.

Finish: The entire cage is rusted lightly and then coated in a dark green flat paint. The painted finish is very rough with the texture provided by the irregular surface of the rust.

## Fake Tip-offs

**1.** There is no sign of wear on the wires wrapped around the base ring. Antiques would be worn flat on each wire.

**2.** This form is not common in the antiques martketplace. View it with suspicion.

*The cages are fastened together by the wrapping and weaving of many fine wires.*

# Varmint Cage                                        164

Thin sheet metal has been woven into a mesh to form a very unique type of cage. The wide strips of metal make this cage very strong, but very dark on the interior. This would seem to be an impractical home for birds. Small animals, on the other hand, would not mind the dark confines of the cage and would find it difficult to break out. The solid bottom pan would provide better containment for the animal's droppings.

The construction techniques and the finish used in its manufacture have made this cage believable as an antique. The London dealer from whom it was originally purchased said that it was made in India.

**Diameter: 18" approx.**
**Height: 16" approx.**

Construction: One of the most interesting things about this cage is the common material size. All the detail parts are made from the same thickness of sheet metal.

The top rounded section is made from a dished, sheet metal top plate that has split strips of sheet metal riveted to its outer edge. These strips are woven into a basket mesh and hammer formed over a shaped block. They are trimmed to size and riveted to the center sheet metal ring. The basket weave is used here to effect the fastening of two strips with one rivet.

To the bottom of the center strip, vertical sheet metal side bars are riveted in place. The side bars are riveted to the vertical flange of the two-piece sheet metal bottom pan. The pan is a crimped flange construction. The door to the cage is fabricated from sheet metal and riveted together.

The only piece that is not sheet metal is the hanging ring on the cage top.

Finish: The sheet metal is pre-corroded and painted a medium green. The rust is allowed to penetrate through the paint, making a great antique look.

### Fake Tip-off

The simulated old finish has no localized wear. The bottom surface would show flats where it has been worn. Around the door and the top ring would be areas of wear as well.

*Blistering of the rust through the paint and the crude construction make a believable antique look.*

# City Hall Birdcage 165

Made of native Philippine wood and steel wire, a fantasy building with Indian architectural features has been created in a birdcage form. It has been designed in three sections. The center section dominates the cage with its high domed and spired top. The construction is simple and naive. There is no great degree of craftsmanship exhibited in the wooden frame or wire screen. A small rectangular clock has been positioned over the main door on the front of the cage. Access to the interior of the cage is by means of a large door inside the main porch on the front. There is a secondary door spring loaded in the middle of the back side. A trap door for the litter pan has been provided at the bottom of the right hand side.

**Overall Height: 31 1/2"**
**Overall Length: 27 1/2"**
**Overall Depth; 13 1/4"**

Construction: The cage assembly is designed and manufactured in five sub-units, each built separately. They are the door and front steps, the main rectangular frame, the two peaked side roofs and the top round domed section. The wooden detail parts are hand cut to shape and size out of soft native woods. Soft low carbon steel wire is used for the cage bars. It is cut to size and hand formed. For the most part it is held in place by insertion into and through the wood frame. However, there are cross wires used for rigidity that are held in place by woven thin wire.

Where rough chipped or broken wooden pieces require fixing, a white putty filler is used and sanded smooth. Small wire nails are used to assemble the wood frame.

Finish: The wood frame is coated with a white primer. The entire cage is then brush finished with an oil base staining coat over the wire and wood.

**Fake Tip-off**

There is no indication of the cage ever being used for birds or anything other than decoration.

*Crude workmanship looks old.*

# Decorative Arts Summary

**M**any countries have supplied the fakes shown in this chapter. I have been told that the paintings of the dogs and chickens have been painted in China. Indonesia, the Philippines, and India have supplied a good portion of the others. Production techniques and finish decorating abilities vary from country to country. They are telltale characteristics that can be used to develop your sixth sense, an ability helpful in determining a piece's authenticity.

The two paintings and the Victorian doll's chair have the common feature of a Biggs label. This clearly tags the three pieces as fakes.

The three cages show definite construction differences. They have been made in three different countries. Knowing that these are fakes, they can be used as a standard for judging other cages. Be sure to examine any piece for reasonable wear and aging of the finish.

The pottery shown all has the common feature of artificial age induced by the Raku type of cooling. The black lined finish is a fake giveaway.

# BIBLIOGRAPHY

Phipps, Francis. Colonial Kitchens, Their Furnishings and Their Gardens.
New York: Hawthorn Books, 1972

D'Allemagne, Henry Rene'. Decorative Antique Ironwork.
New York: Dover Publications, 1968

Lindsay, J. Seymour. Iron and Brass Implements of the English House.
London: Alec Tiranti, 1970

Sonn, Albert H. Early American Wrought Iron.
New York: Bonanza Books, 1979

Thwing, Leroy. Flickering Flames.
Rutland, Vermont: Charles E. Tuttle Co., 1972

Rushlight Club. Early Lighting,
Boston, Massachusetts, 1979

Kaye, Myrna. Yankee Weathervanes.
New York: E.P. Dutton and Co., 1975

Westervelt, A.B. and W.T. American Antique Weathervanes.
New York: Dover Publication, 1982

Fitzgerald, Ken. Weathervanes and Whiligigs.
New York: Clarkson N. Potter, 1967

Lynch, Kenneth. Weathervanes.
Canterbury, Connecticut: Canterbury Publishing, 1971

Klamkin, Charles. Weathervanes.
New York: Hawthorn Books, 1973

Miller, Steve. The Art of the Weathervane.
Exton, Pennsylvania: Schiffer Publishing Co., 1984

Richardson, M.T. Practical Blacksmithing.
New York: Weathervane Books, 1978

Nutting, Wallace. Furniture Treasury.
New York: The Macmillan Co., 1948

Hayward, Arthur H. Colonial Lighting.
Boston, Massachusetts: B.J. Brimmer Co., 1923

# GLOSSARY

ALLIGATORED FINISH - A cracked paint finish that resembles the skin of an alligator.

BALL-PEEN HAMMER - A hammer having a hemispherical peen for beating metal.

BRAZING - To unite metal objects by bonding together, with a high melting point, brass base solder.

BURR - A protruding, ragged metal edge raised on a surface in drilling or shearing.

CANDELABRA - Ornamental branched holders for more than one candle.

CARBON BLACK - Any of various finely divided forms of amorphous carbon used in pigments.

CHANDELIER - A light fixture suspended from a ceiling.

COLD CHISEL - A steel chisel used on cold metal.

CRIMPED SEAMS - To fold the edges of sheet metal to make a lock seam.

DEBURR - To remove the ragged edge left by drilling or shearing metal.

ELECTRIC WELDING - A process used to unite pieces of steel using electricity to provide the heat for melting.

FAKE - To make something deceptive or fraudulent. In antiques, duplicating both form and age.

FLEUR-DE-LIS - A heraldic device somewhat resembling three petals or floral segments of an iris tied by an encircling band.

FLOOR STANDARD - An upright or supporting part of a floor standing lighting device.

FONT - The reservoir for oil in a lamp.

FORGE WELDING - The bonding of two or more pieces of iron using heat and hammering to form the joint.

FORGING - The forming of metal using heat and hammering.

GALLING - The distortion and abrasion of a bearing surface.

GAME CROWN - An iron rack used to hang game in a larder and shaped like a crown.

GAS WELDING - A process used to unite pieces of steel using the gases oxygen and burning acetelyne to provide heat.

GEORGIAN - The period of British history from 1714 to 1830.

HOG SCRAPER - A tin candlestick that has a round base once used to scrape bristles off hog hides.

HOT ROLLED - A process of roll forming steel sheet using heat.

JAM NUT - A thin nut generally used to lock another nut in place.

JAPANNING - A coating of various hard black varnishes on metal, originally from Japan.

MAKE-DO - A useful item made from the broken parts of other.

MILL FINISH - The surface finish on metal as it comes from the manufacturer.

MILL SCALE - Corrosion left on the metal surface after the hot rolling process.

PENNY FEET - The penny shaped feet of metal items.

PLASTIC BODY FILLER - A two part resin mixture used to form fillets and smooth rough surfaces.

PLUG WELD - A small circular weld.

PRESS FIT - A tight mechanical fit used to fasten pieces together.

PRIMER - A surface coating used to protect the surface and prepare it for a final finish.

PRODUCTION LOT - A group that was produced as part of a normal manufacturing process.

RAKU - A Japanese glaze firing process.

RAT TAIL - A piece of metal forged to a thin tapered shape.

REPRODUCTION - A duplication of the original's form. Does not attempt to replicate age.

RIVET - A metal pin for passing through holes in two or more pieces to hold them together, usually with a head at one end while the other end is hammered.

ROLL PIN - A roll-formed piece of steel that when forced into a hole, maintains a tight fit due to the spring action of its roll form.

ROSEMALING - Norwegian decorative painting on wood.

RUSH LIGHT - Grease soaked marsh rushes are used as fuel for this lighting device.

SCONCE - A bracket for candles or other lights, placed on a wall or mirror.

SOLDER - Various soft alloys fused and applied to the joint between metal objects to unite them without heating them to the melting point.

STAINING WAX - A pigmented wax used to prematurely age finishes.

STEEL - Any various forms of modified iron, artificially produced, having a carbon content less than that of pig iron and more than that of wrought iron.

TEN PENNY NAIL - A nail three inches in length.

TIN - Another name for tinplate, iron or steel sheet coated with tin.

TRAMMEL - A device hung in a fireplace used to adjust the height of pots and kettles over a fire.

WEATHERCOCK - A weathervane in the shape of a cock.

WELDING WIRE - The metal melted in the process of electric welding with a wire feed welding machine.

WELDMENT - The assembly that results from the welding of two or more pieces together.

VETTING - To appraise or verify for authenticity.

# INDEX